African Anarchism
The History of a Movement

by

Sam Mbah & I.E. Igariwey

See Sharp Press ◆ Tucson, Arizona ◆ 1997

For information contact See Sharp Press, P.O. Box 1731,
Tucson, AZ 85702-1731.

Mbah, Sam.
        African anarchism : the history of a movement / Sam Mbah
& I.E. Igariwey. – Tucson, AZ : See Sharp Press, c1997.

        128 p. ; 23 cm.
        Includes bibliographical references and index.
        ISBN 1-884365-05-1

        1. Anarchism - Africa. 2. Socialism - Africa. 3. Tanzania -
Politics and government - 1964 4. Guinea-Bissau - Politics and
government - 1974 5. Ghana - Politics and government - 1979-
6. Nigeria - Politics and government - 1960- 7. South Africa - Politics
and government - 1948- I. Title II. Igariwey, I. E.

                        320.96032

Cover design by Clifford Harper. Interior design by Chaz Bufe. Printed on
acid-free paper with soy-based ink by Thomson-Shore, Inc., Dexter, Michigan.

Contents

Foreword i

Preface iii

1. What Is Anarchism? 1

   definitions; attitudes toward capitalism, the state, religion, and other hierarchical institutions; positive aspects—voluntary cooperation, mutual aid, decentralization, horizontal organization, individual autonomy; what anarchism is not (chaos, terrorism); origins of anarcho-syndicalism

2. Anarchism in History 18

   Marx and Bakunin; the First International; disagreement over the role of the state; relationship to syndicalism and guild socialism

3. Anarchistic Precedents in Africa 27

   anarchic elements in African traditional societies; African communalism; political organization under communalism; administration of justice; traditional religions; age grades; secret societies; eonomic aspects; work specialization, trade, and the breakdown of communalism; stateless societies in Africa; the Igbo; the Niger Delta peoples; the Tallensi; colonialism and the incorporation of Africa into the world capitalist economy; economic aspects of colonialism; the colonial educational system; class formation in post-colonial Africa; function of different classes in post-colonial economies; African socialism; is there an African anarchism?; anarchistic elements in African socialism—Julius Nyerere and Ujamaa; anarchist groups in South Africa and Nigeria

4. The Development of Socialism in Africa 54

   class formation under colonialism; cooptation of local leaders; the trade union movement and the liberation struggle in Africa; the Nigerian labor union movement; lack of revolutionary perspective in Nigerian labor unions; the South African labor movement; foundation of Communist Party in South Africa; the "revolution" in Guinea; Sekou Toure and the Democratic Party of Guinea; the Awareness League in Nigeria

5. The Failure of Socialism in Africa 72
ideology and economic development; failure of Guinean "revolution"; lessons
from Guinean failure; Tanzania, Julius Nyerere and Ujamaa socialism; reasons
for failure of Ujamaa socialism; additional failures of "African socialism"—
Ethiopia, Burkina Faso; state capitalism and instability; one-party ideologies and
depoliticization; military interventions and their effects; political corruption and
social instability—case studies of Ghana and Nigeria; the IMF's structural
adjustment programs (SAPs), electoralism, and Africa's future; economic and
social effects of SAPs; constitutional conventions; the human rights question;
repression in Nigeria, Libya, Ghana, and Zimbabwe

6. Obstacles to the Development of Anarchism in Africa 94
colonial education and its aftermath; the Western-style legal system; the military;
ethnic versus class consciousness; religious and cultural factors; the need for
international solidarity

7. Anarchism's Future in Africa 101
anarchism in a world context; the crises of capitalism and marxist "socialism";
Africa's dire economic situation; anarchism and the national question;
anarchism—the only way out for Africa

Bibliography 109
Index 112

Foreword

This first-of-its-kind book should be of use to everyone with an interest in either Africa or anarchism. Authors Sam Mbah and I.E. Igariwey begin by lucidly explaining the basic principles and practices of anarchism. After outlining what anarchism is and is not, they go on to compare anarchism's principles and practices to those of other social-change ideologies, specifically to marxist socialism.

The authors then move on to Africa, exploring at length the "anarchistic elements" in many traditional (pre-colonial) African societies. Next they examine the devastating effects of colonialism on Africa's traditional societies and on Africa's economic and political structures, as well as the horrendous problems left in the wake of colonialism: underdeveloped, debt-ridden dependent economies with huge disparities between rich and poor; violent ethnic antagonisms caused by the deliberate setting of ethnic group against ethnic group, and by the creation of artificial national boundaries; and European-style governments, legal and educational systems, and military forces, all quite unsuited to African conditions.

Following this, the authors go on to examine the failed attempts at social change by "African socialist" governments in the post-colonial period, with special attention to Julius Nyerere's Tanzania, Sekou Toure's Guinea, and Kwame Nkrumah's Ghana. The unfortunate conclusion they arrive at is that a humane, fundamental reconstruction of society is impossible in Africa, as elsewhere, via government.

This is not a hopeless conclusion, however, as the authors state that there *is* a way out for Africa—an anarchist reconstruction of its economic and social structures. They also point out that because of the many similarities between anarchist beliefs and practices and those of traditional African societies (which still survive to some extent), Africa seems the most likely of all the continents to witness a true social revolution—a revolution in an industrial age based on the "anarchist elements" in traditional African societies.

On a more personal note, I should apologize to any readers who find a few minor loose ends in this book. There is a reason for this: the authors live in Enugu, Nigeria, and communication with them has been difficult to say the least. (Whether this has been due to inefficiencies in the Nigerian postal and telephone services, or due to deliberate interference by the Nigerian government, I can't say.) As a result of this problem, it has been impossible to check on a number of minor details, such as first names of a few persons mentioned in the text. Ultimately, I decided it was better to publish the book with a few minor loose ends rather than wait months if not years to contact the authors about these matters.

As a final note, I should also apologize to any readers who might find the title of this book inappropriate. When I accepted this book for publication, I accepted it on the basis of a good topic, good cover letter, and good proposal. The deadline to announce the coming season's titles was fast approaching, so I assigned the book an ISBN (International Standard Book Number), announced it, and commissioned Cliff Harper to do the cover. At that point, for all practical purposes, the book's title was set in stone. When the manuscript arrived, I discovered that it was not in fact a history, but something more valuable—a forward-looking book concerned with achieving positive social change. A more fitting title for this valuable book would be *African Anarchism: Prospects for the Future*.

—Chaz Bufe
Publisher,
See Sharp Press

Preface

Though not abundant anywhere, anarchist literature is especially scarce in Africa. This fact, in part, explains why anarchist ideas are not spreading as fast as they should in Africa and elsewhere, in spite of the crisis of state socialism.

Anarchist development has also been retarded for decades for other reasons, including the theoretical weakness of anarchism. However historically correct anarchist positions might be, without a rigorous theoretical foundation, most workers, peasants and other potential anarchists will remain indifferent to the philosophy.

It's true that anarchists were among the first to put forward accurate critiques of capitalism and of marxist socialism, warning about where the statist path would ultimately lead. And anarchists also developed superior methods of organization based on genuine mass democracy. The point, however, is that in their critique of marxism, anarchists have failed to explain in sufficient depth the authoritarian side of marxism, and why that authoritarian side is a fatal flaw.

It is against this background that we, members of the Awareness League, have elected to trace the relationship between Africa and anarchism. In doing so, we are impelled by a two-fold sense of historical responsibility: to enrich anarchism and anarchist principles with an African perspective, and to carve out a place for Africa within the framework of the worldwide anarchist movement. There can be little doubt—given the collapse of the authoritarian left—that the time is ripe for this project. But in a world suffused with capitalist and, to a lesser degree, marxist influences—from patterns of childhood socialization to the mass media's stranglehold on public opinion—the anarchist project faces an uphill climb. This book is our contribution to this daunting task.

This work highlights the opportunities that exist for anarchism, analyzing the concrete challenges that lie ahead. Chapters one and two deal with the history, growth and development of anarchism, from the fierce struggle between Karl Marx and Mikhail Bakunin and their followers within the First International to the Spanish Revolution.

Chapter three unravels the origins of anarchism on the African continent, identifying certain "anarchic elements" in African communalism and analyzing the social organization of stateless societies in Africa. It traces incorporation of African economies into the world capitalist system and poses the question, "Is there an African anarchism?" Chapter four examines the development of socialism in Africa. Chapter five deals with the failure of socialism and its implications for anarchism in Africa. Chapter six analyzes in detail current drawbacks to the realization of anarchist ideals in Africa. And chapter seven details the ways in which anarchism represents the best, and indeed the only, way forward for Africa.

This work would not have been possible but for the encouragement, solidarity, support and assistance—material and moral—of the International Workers Association (IWA) and its affiliates in Europe and the United States. Special mention must, however, be made of Jose "Pepe" Jiminez, general secretary of the IWA, Mitch Miller of the Workers Solidarity Alliance (U.S. IWA affiliate), Bob McGlynn of Neither East Nor West (USA), Monika Grosche of FAU (German IWA affiliate), Lourdes Redondo Ramajo (Asociación Internacional de los Trabajadores—Spain), members of the Workers Solidarity Movement (Ireland), the French section of the IWA, and others too numerous to mention by name. We are similarly indebted to all members of the Awareness League in Nigeria, who contributed directly and indirectly to making this work a reality. Finally, Lynea Search also deserves thanks for doing a fine editing job.

—Sam Mbah & I.E. Igariwey

1

What Is Anarchism?

Anarchism as a social philosophy, theory of social organization, and social movement is remote to Africa—indeed, almost unknown. It is underdeveloped in Africa as a systematic body of thought, and largely unknown as a revolutionary movement. Be that as it may, anarchism as a way of life is not at all new to Africa, as we shall see. The continent's earliest contact with European anarchist thought probably did not take place before the second half of the 20th century, with the single exception of South Africa. It is, therefore, to Western thinkers that we must turn for an elucidation of anarchism.

Anarchism derives not so much from abstract reflections of intellectuals or philosophers as from the objective conditions in which workers and producers find themselves. Though one can find traces of it earlier, anarchism as a revolutionary philosophy arose as part of the worldwide socialist movement in the 19th century. The dehumanizing nature of capitalism and the state system stimulated the desire to build a better world—a world rooted in true equality, liberty, freedom and solidarity. The tyrannical propensities of the state—any state—underpinned by private capital, have propelled anarchists to insist on the complete abolition of the state system.

The New Encyclopaedia Britannica[1] (15th Edition) characterizes anarchism as a social philosophy "whose central tenet is that human beings can live justly and harmoniously without government and that the imposition of government upon human beings is in fact harmful and evil." Similarly, *The Encyclopedia Americana*[2] (International Edition) describes anarchism as a theory of social organization "that looks upon all law and government as invasive, the twin sources of nearly all social evils. It therefore advocates the abolition of all government as the term is understood today, except that originating in voluntary cooperation." Anarchists, it goes on to say, do not conceive of a society without order, "but the order they visualize arises out of voluntary association, preferably through self-governing groups." For its part *Collier's Encyclopedia*[3] conceives anarchism as a 19th-century movement "holding the belief that society should be controlled entirely by voluntarily organized groups and not by the political state." Coercion, according to this line of reasoning, is to be dispensed with in order that "each individual may attain his most complete development." As far as definitions go, these lend some useful, if superficial, insights into anarchist doctrine. But their usefulness in the elucidation of the rich and expansive body of thought known as anarchism is patently limited. The wide gamut of anarchist theory is revealed only in the writings of anarchists themselves, as well as in the writings of a few nonanarchists.

According to Bertrand Russell, anarchism "is the theory which is opposed to every kind of forcible government. It is opposed to the state as the embodiment of the force employed in the government of the community. Such government as anarchism can tolerate must be free government, not merely in the sense that it is that of a majority, but in the sense that it is assented to by all. Anarchists object to such institutions as the police and the criminal law, by means of which the will of one part of the community is forced upon another part. . . . Liberty is the supreme good in the anarchist creed, and liberty is sought by the direct road of abolishing all forcible control over the individual by the community."[4]

Russell justifies the anarchist demand for the abolition of government, including government by majority rule, writing, "it is undeniable, that the rule of a majority may be almost as hostile to freedom as the rule of a minority: the divine right of majorities is a dogma as little possessed of absolute truth as any other."[5]

Likewise, anarchism is irreconcilably opposed to capitalism as well as to government. It advocates direct action by the working class to abolish the capitalist order, including all state institutions. In place of state/capitalist institutions and value systems, anarchists work to establish a social order based on individual freedom, voluntary co-operation, and self-managed productive communities.

Toward this end, anarchism posits that every activity currently performed by the state and its institutions could be better handled by voluntary or associative effort, and that no restraint upon conduct is required because of the natural tendency of people in a state of freedom to respect each other's rights.

Anarchists are so implacably opposed to the state system and its manifestations that one of the founding fathers of anarchism, Pierre-Joseph Proudhon, proclaimed: "Governments are the scourge of God." Mikhail Bakunin elaborated on Proudhon's propositions, explaining the goal of anarchism as the full development of all human beings in conditions of liberty and equality:

> It is the triumph of humanity, it is the conquest and accomplishment of the full freedom and full development, material, intellectual and moral, of every individual, by the absolutely free and spontaneous organization of economic and social solidarity as completely as possible between all human beings living on the earth.[6]

Bakunin goes on to say that "we understand by liberty, on the one hand, the development, as complete as possible, of all the natural faculties of each individual and, on the other hand, his independence, not as regards natural and social laws but as regards all the laws imposed by other human wills, whether collective or separate. . . . What we want is the abolition of artificial privilege, legal, official influences."[7]

Such privileges are necessarily the prerogative of the state. And thus Bakunin characterizes the state as nothing but domination, oppression, and exploitation, "regularized" and "systematized":

> The state is government from above downwards of an immense number of men, very different from the point of view of the degree of their culture, the nature of the countries or localities that they inhabit, the occupation they follow, the interests and the aspirations directing them—the state is the government of all those by some or other minority; this minority, even if it were a thousand times elected by universal suffrage and controlled in its acts by popular institutions, unless it were endowed with the omniscience, omnipresence and omnipotence which the theologians attribute to God, it is impossible that it could know and foresee the needs or satisfy with an even justice the most legitimate and pressing interests in the world. There will always be discontented people because there will always be some who are sacrificed.[8]

As Bakunin further observes, the state was an historically necessary evil, but its complete extinction will be, sooner or later, equally necessary. He repudiates all laws, including those made under universal suffrage, arguing that freedom does not mean equal access to coercive power (i.e., government via "free" elections), but rather that it means freedom *from* coercive power—in other words, one becomes really free only when, and in proportion as, all others are free.

It is Peter Kropotkin, however, who provides both systematic and penetrating insight into anarchism as a practical political and social philosophy. In two seminal essays, *Anarchism* and *Anarchist Communism*, he declares that the private ownership of land, capital and machinery has had its time and shall come to an end, with the transformation of all factors of production into common social property, to be managed in common by the producers of wealth. Under this dispensation, the individual reclaims his/her full liberty of initiative and action through participation in freely constituted groups and federations, that will come to satisfy all the varied needs of human beings. "The ultimate aim of society is the reduction of the functions of government to nil—[that] is, to a society without government, to Anarchy."[9]

He elaborates:

You cannot modify the existing conditions of property without deeply modifying at the same time the political organization. You must limit the powers of government and renounce parliamentary rule. To each new economical phase of life corresponds a new political phase. Absolute monarchy—that is, court-rule—corresponded to the system of serfdom. Representative government corresponds to capital-rule. Both, however, are class-rule.

But in a society where the distinction between capitalist and laborer has disappeared, there is no need of such a government; it would be an anachronism, a nuisance. Free workers would require a free organization, and this cannot have another basis than free agreement and free cooperation, without sacrificing the autonomy of the individual to the all-pervading interference of the state. The no-capitalist system implies the no-government system. Meaning thus the emancipation of man from the oppressive power of capitalist and government as well, the system of Anarchy becomes a synthesis of the two powerful currents of thought which characterize our century.[10]

Kropotkin posits that representative government (democracy) has accomplished its historical mission to the extent that it delivered a mortal blow to court-rule (absolute monarchy). And since each economic phase in history necessarily involves its own political phase, it is impossible to eliminate the basis of present economic life, namely private property, without a corresponding change in political organization.[11] Conceived thus, anarchism becomes the synthesis of the two chief desires of humanity since the dawn of history: economic freedom and political freedom.

An excursion into history reveals that the state has always been the property of one privileged class or another: a priestly class, an aristocratic class, a capitalist class, and, finally, a bureaucratic (or "new") class, as in the Soviet Union and China. The existence of a privileged class is absolutely necessary for the preservation of the state. "Every logical and sincere theory of the state," Bakunin asserts, "is essentially founded on the principle of *authority*—that is to say, on the eminently theological, metaphysical and political idea that the masses, always incapable of governing themselves, must submit at all times to the benevolent yoke . . . which in one way or another, is imposed on them from above."[12]

This phenomenon is the virtual equivalent of slavery—a practice with deep statist roots. This is illustrated by the following passage from Kropotkin:

> We cry out against the feudal barons who did not permit anyone to settle on the land otherwise than on payment of one quarter of the crops to the lord of the manor; but we continue to do as they did —we extend their system. The forms have changed, but the essence has remained the same."[13]

Bakunin expresses this thought even more poignantly:

> Slavery can change its form and its name—its basis remains the same. This basis is expressed by the words: being a slave is being forced to work for other people—as being a master is to live on the labor of other people. In ancient times as today in Asia and Africa, slaves were simply called slaves. In the Middle Ages, they took the name of "serfs," today they are called "wage-earners." The position of the latter is much more honorable and less hard than that of slaves, but they are nonetheless forced by hunger, as well as by the

political and social institutions, to maintain by very hard work the absolute or relative idleness of others. Consequently, they are slaves. And, in general, no state, either ancient or modern, has ever been able, or ever will be able, to do without the forced labor of the masses, whether wage-earners or slaves."[14]

The primary distinguishing factor between the wage worker and the slave is, perhaps, that the wage worker has some capacity to withdraw his or her labor while the slave cannot.

G. P. Maximoff does not see things any differently. To him, the essence of anarchism consists of the abolition of private property relations and the state system, the principal agent of capital. He states that "capitalism in its present stage has reached the full maturity of imperialism . . . beyond this point, the road of capitalism is the road of deterioration."[15]

But capitalism is not alone here. Marxist state socialism as expressed in the former Soviet Union, from its very inception, provided ample evidence for the anarchist argument. Says Maximoff:

The Russian Revolution . . . revealed the nature of state socialism and its mechanism, demonstrating that there is no great difference in principle between a state socialist and a bourgeois society . . . between these societies, seemingly so irreconcilable and so antagonistic to each other, there is really only a quantitative, not a qualitative, difference. And the attempt to solve the social problem by utilizing the methods inherent in rigid, logically consistent power communism, as in the Russian Revolution, demonstrates that even quantity is not always on the side of authoritarian communism and that, on the contrary, when logically pursued to the end, it resembles despotism in many ways.[16]

Thus, says Maximoff, anarchism is the only social force capable of destroying private property and its mainstay, the state; of establishing public ownership and a stateless, federalist organization of society on the basis of the free association of productive units both in factories and towns. Anarchism alone "can assure liberty, i.e., the well-being and the free development of the individual in society, and of society itself. It alone will stop the division of society into classes and will abolish every possibility of the exploitation or rule of man by man."[17]

The International Workers Association[18] (IWA) is a federation of anarchist labor groups in dozens of countries around the world. While it terms its goals "revolutionary syndicalist," they are in fact virtually identical with anarchist goals. The IWA's statutes state in part:

> Revolutionary syndicalism is the pronounced enemy of all economic and social monopoly. It aims at the abolition of privilege by the establishing of economic communes and administrative organs run by the workers in the fields and factories, forming a system of free councils without subordination to any power or political party. Revolutionary Syndicalism poses as an alternative to the politics of states and parties, the economic reorganization of production. It is opposed to the governing of people by others and poses self-management as an alternative.
>
> Consequently, the goal of revolutionary syndicalism is not the conquest of political power, but the abolition of all state functions in the life of society. Revolutionary Syndicalism considers that the disappearance of the monopoly of property must also be accompanied by the disappearance of all forms of domination. Statism, however camouflaged, can never be an instrument for human liberation and, on the contrary, will always be the creator of new monopolies and privileges.

Based on the foregoing, we may summarize the theoretical aspects of anarchism: anarchism seeks the abolition of capitalism and the capitalist mode of production—this includes the social relations it engenders, its market processes, and the commodity and wage systems. This is not possible to accomplish, however, without the simultaneous abolition of the state system together with its value systems and institutions, including the legal and school systems, mass media, bureaucracy, police, patriarchal family, organized religion, etc.

The state system is, of course, neither peculiar to nor exclusive to capitalism; it is also a cardinal feature of state socialism, that is, marxist socialism as represented by both the Soviet and Chinese systems. And the state system everywhere displays the same authoritarian and hierarchical features that serve to circumscribe the freedom of the individual, and thus that of society at large.

Anarchism derives from the class struggle engendered by the enslavement of workers and from their historical aspirations toward freedom. Class in this sense is not just an economic concept, nor does it relate merely to the ownership of the means of production: it in fact represents the unwholesome amount of power which a tiny group wields and exercises over the rest of society.

The instrument of this tiny elite, the state, is simultaneously the organized violence of the owning class and the system of its executive will. As the Dielo Trouda group further puts it, authority is always dependent on the exploitation and enslavement of the majority of the people. And authority without hierarchy, without exploitation and loss of freedom, loses its reason for being. "The state and authority take from the masses all initiative, kill the spirit of creation and free activity, cultivate in them the servile psychology of submission."[19]

The strength of anarchism is predicated on the fact that humans throughout history have been propelled by the quest for equality and liberty, liberty being indivisible from equality, and vice versa. This desire seems to stem from the fact that human beings are basically cooperative rather than competitive.

In place of a society organized along class lines, marked by hierarchy and authority, anarchism advocates a self-managed, self-reliant society based on cooperative, voluntary mutual aid and association, and devoid of government (i.e., coercion). In such a society the ownership of the means of production is not the exclusive preserve of any individual or group, and wage labor is nonexistent, allowing the individual ample freedom and initiative for full development. "There will be no demi-gods, but there will also be no slaves. Demi-gods and slaves will both become men; the former will have to step down from their Olympian heights, the latter will have to move up considerably."[20] In the broad sweep of history, anarchism will take its place as a social order founded on and geared toward a post-capitalist, post-government society.

Importantly, anarchism does *not* imply the absence of organization. In contrast to the irrational, hierarchical, centralized authority of government and corporations, anarchists accept and indeed respect the rational authority of the expert—an authority of a different type: one based upon expertise and experience, not coercive power.

Anarchists have always recognized the need for organization. For them, however, the question is what type of organization. Anarchists argue for horizontal organization based on decentralization, individual and local autonomy, social equality, and democratic decision making.

Ultimately, anarchism rejects all struggle for state (political) power, holding out as its weapon and method the social struggle of workers and peasants based in solidarity and internationalism. Consequently, the task of emancipating working people must be the work of working people themselves. This emancipation consists of the reduction of the functions of government to zero, ensuring that, at all times, control over all necessary forms of social organization is from below.

WHAT ANARCHISM IS NOT

Unfortunately, in addition to saying what anarchism *is*, it's also necessary to say what it is *not*. It's necessary to address the vulgar misconceptions and deliberate, outright distortions that marxists and capitalist apologists propagate about anarchism.

By far the greatest misconception is that anarchism is synonymous with rejection of order or with a state of disorder, involving chaos, destruction, and violence. Nothing could be further from the truth. Kevin Doyle, of *Workers Solidarity* magazine writes, "Anarchism has been deliberately slandered and misrepresented, not only by those running [this] society, but also by most on the left. Deliberately, for the reason that its uncompromising and radical critique of society and how to change it poses a challenge that cannot be met except by slander. Its roots and association with the working class of all countries tells the real truth."[21]

Anarchism is basically opposed to violence, and to disorder, chaos and terrorism as well. Anarchists the world over uphold peace as an overriding value and, consequently, reject war, armies, militarism, and the development and acquisition of technologies that promote war. Anarchists advocate violence only as a form of self-defense.

The statutes of the International Workers Association put the issue in sharp perspective: "While revolutionary syndicalism is opposed to all organized violence of the state, it realizes that there will be extremely violent clashes during the decisive struggles between the capitalism of today and the free communism of tomorrow. Consequently, it recognizes as valid that violence which can be used as a means of defense against the violent methods used by the ruling classes during the social revolution."[22]

Rejection of aggressive violence and terrorism does not, however, make anarchists pacifists. On the contrary, a successful anarchist movement will face state violence. The way to combat this repressive violence is not through terrorism or through the creation of hierarchical military organizations, but through the creation of community-based defense and educational organizations that are willing to defend their own social structures.

Anarchist advocacy of defensive organizations was born out of a historical recognition of the state as the most brutal and ruthless agent of terror, and the recognition that its use of violence depends almost entirely on the degree to which it feels challenged. Anarchists recognize that the state will do anything, no matter how vile, to maintain its own power.

As for anarchism and terrorism, only a tiny minority of anarchists have taken part in terrorist activities. This is because anarchists recognize that means determine ends, and because they seek to abolish the state system, not to establish a vanguard that would aspire to state power. As the anonymous authors of *You Can't Blow Up a Social Relationship: The Anarchist Case Against Terrorism* put it:

> You can't blow up a social relationship. The total collapse of this society would provide no guarantee about what replaced it. Unless a majority of people had the ideas and organization sufficient for the creation of an alternative society, we would see the old world reassert itself because it is what people would be used to, what they believed in, what existed unchallenged in their own personalities.
>
> Proponents of terrorism and guerrillaism are to be opposed because their actions are vanguardist and authoritarian, because their ideas, to the extent that they are substantial, are wrong or unrelated to the results of their actions (especially when they call themselves libertarians or anarchists), because their killing cannot be justified, and finally because their actions produce either repression with nothing in return, or an authoritarian regime.[23]

Bertrand Russell adds:

> In its general doctrines, there is nothing [in anarchism] essentially involving violent methods or a virulent hatred of the rich . . . The revolt against law naturally leads, except in those who are controlled by a real passion for humanity, to a relaxation of all the usually accepted moral values. It would be wholly unfair to judge anarchist doctrine, or the views of its leading exponents, by such phenomena. . . . This must be remembered in exculpation of the authorities and the thoughtless public, who often confound in a common

detestation the parasites of the movement and the truly heroic and high-minded men who have elaborated its theories and sacrificed comfort and success to their propagation.[24]

L.S. Bevington sums it all up:

Of course we know that among those who call themselves anarchists, there are a minority of unbalanced enthusiasts who look upon every illegal and sensational act of violence as a matter for hysterical jubilation. Very useful to the police and the press, unsteady in intellect and of weak moral principle, they have repeatedly shown themselves accessible to venal considerations. They, and their violence, and their professed anarchism are purchasable, and in the last resort they are welcome and efficient partisans of the [ruling class] . . . Let us leave indiscriminate killing and injuring to the government—to its statesmen, its stockbrokers, its officers, and its law.[25]

Anarchism in its present manifestations as revolutionary syndicalism, anarcho-syndicalism, and anarcho-communism, advocates direct action, but not terrorism or violent acts.

Similarly, anarchism does not imply the absence of organization. As mentioned previously, anarchists reject the hierarchical and authoritarian model of organization that erodes freedom and equality; but they do not reject the horizontal model of organization based on democratic decision-making, decentralization, voluntary association, and voluntary cooperation. Indeed, this form of organization is central to the anarchist vision.

Concerning religion, Bakunin's *God and the State* exposed the integral relationship between the church and the state system. It states, "God moving in the world has made the state possible,"[26] in tracing this connection: "It is necessary to think of it [the state] not merely as a given state or a particular institution, but of its essence or idea as a real manifestation of God. Every state, of whatever kind it may be, partakes of this divine essence."

Organized religion is indeed one of the pillars of capitalist social relationships. It embodies similar hierarchical and authoritarian features as the state and the corporation, and its ideology and institutions are just as antithetical to the individual's quest for freedom and equality.

It should be understood, though, that some people who profess anarchist beliefs nonetheless still hold some type of religious belief. This may seem contradictory to nonreligious anarchists, but the sincerity of many of these people is unquestionable.

So, what is wrong with religion from the anarchist point of view? In addition to their hierarchical and authoritarian features, patriarchal religions dominate through the induction of fear and irrationality, and thus rob people of self-determination and the ability to think clearly. As well, they have very pronounced intrusive tendencies. Many of the worst intrusive excesses of governments, both ancient and modern, have been the direct result of attempts by religious partisans to legislate "morality"—and to enforce that "morality" at the point of a sword or gun.

Still, most anarchists would agree with the statement of the Geneva section to the Brussels Congress of the International Workingmen's Association, which says that "religious thought, as a product of the individual mind, is untouchable as long as it does not become a public activity."[27] Unfortunately, because of the intrusive, authoritarian nature of almost all organized religions, it's rare that religious beliefs remain a private matter. Thus, most anarchists oppose religion.

ORIGINS OF ANARCHO-SYNDICALISM

The word *anarchism* is derived from two Greek words, "an" and "archos," meaning "without rule" or "contrary to authority."

The true origins of anarchist principles date far back in time. Conceived as a way of life or a philosophy which is opposed to every form of government or forcible state control over the individual, anarchism has been a familiar theme for humankind from the dawn of history.

In ancient Greece, Zeno (342–267? B.C.E.), the leading light of Stoic philosophy, vehemently opposed the idea of the state's omnipotence, its intervention in the life of and its regimentation of the individual in society. He consequently proclaimed the moral law of the individual. According to him, although humanity's self-preservation instincts can lead to egotism, nature has supplied a corrective to it by instilling the instinct of sociability: "When men are reasonable enough to follow their natural instincts, they will unite across the frontiers and constitute the Cosmos. They will have no need of law-courts or police, they will have no temples and no public worship, and use no money—free gifts taking the place of exchanges."[28]

Similar ideas lie buried in the writings and thoughts of several subsequent philosophers and thinkers up to medieval times. It is highly probable that anarchist ideas have been equally pervasive in Africa.

In his seminal work, *An Enquiry Concerning Political Justice*, William Godwin in 1793 anticipated later anarchist principles, although he did not employ the term anarchism. His pioneering work yielded an outline of a decentralized and nonhierarchical society; he advocated the abolition of every form of government. He further called for "the progressive breaking down of all institutions that contribute to coercion and inequality. . . . Future organizations would be loose and voluntary associations." A society could perfectly well exist without any government, he concluded; such communities would be small and perfectly autonomous. With regard to property, he declared that the right of everyone "to every substance capable of contributing to the benefit of a human being must be regulated only by justice; the substance must go to him who most wants it."[29]

Godwin rejected laws, all laws, because the remedy they offer is worse than the evils they pretend to cure.

It was not, however, until the publication in 1840 of French writer Pierre-Joseph Proudhon's *What Is Property?* that modern anarchism emerged as a force in social thought. Proudhon rejected law and authority in all their ramifications, and for the first time adopted the word anarchism as a positive term. He advocated a society without government, and used the word "anarchy" to describe it.

In a subsequent book, *The Federation Principle*, published in 1863, Proudhon elaborated slightly upon his earlier theory of government, favoring the formation of self-governing communities. He found in communism no redeeming feature, preferring instead "anarchist individualism." He advocated an economic system of "mutualism," which seeks to rob capital of its capacity to earn interest. It is based on "the reciprocal confidence of all those engaged in production, who agree to exchange among themselves produce at cost value."[30] Other advocates of mutualism include Josiah Warren in the United States and William Thompson in England.

Anarchism as a social movement didn't really emerge, however, until the appearance of Mikhail Bakunin. Born on May 30, 1814 of

Russian nobility, Bakunin early in life abandoned his military commission and delved instead into philosophy, a preoccupation that brought him into contact with Karl Marx, Arnold Ruge, Wilhelm Weitling, Pierre-Joseph Proudhon, George Sand, and Friedrich Engels. His activities brought him repeatedly into conflict with the Czarist government. Weitling's ideas of a society administered without government, with obligations but without laws, and with corrections instead of punishments, had a lasting influence on Bakunin, as did the ideas of Proudhon. As for Karl Marx, Bakunin attested to the German thinker's real genius, scholarship, and revolutionary zeal, but was repelled by his arrogance and egotism.[31]

In Italy in 1864 Bakunin founded the International Fraternity or Alliance of Socialist Revolutionaries. By 1867, he had moved to Switzerland where he played an important role in the founding of the International Alliance of Socialist Democracy. The Alliance's program provides an insight into Bakunin's initial ideas. It reads in part:

> The Alliance declares itself atheist; it desires the definitive and entire abolition of classes, and [favors] the political equality and social equalization of individuals of both sexes. It desires that the earth, the instruments of labor, like other capital, become the collective property of society as a whole, shall no longer be utilized except by the workers, that is to say, by agricultural and industrial associations. It recognizes that all actually existing political and authoritarian states, reducing themselves more and more to the mere administrative functions of the public services in their respective countries, must disappear in the universal union of free associations, both agricultural and industrial.[32]

Unlike Marx, Bakunin did not clearly set forth his vision of an ideal society. His best known work, *God and the State*, is a biting, insightful attack on government and religion; in it, he states that "belief in God and belief in the state [are] the two great obstacles to human liberty." But he does not present a systematic exposition of an alternative to capitalist/statist society.

While Bakunin remains perhaps the most revered figure in anarchism, it fell to those who followed him, notably Peter Kropotkin Rudolf Rocker, and Murray Bookchin, to espouse clearly, systematically, and profoundly the essential ideas on the form, structure and content of an anarchist society. Among Kropotkin's many works,

Fields, Factories and Workshops Tomorrow, The Conquest of Bread, Anarchism, and *Anarchist Communism* stand out.

In the the first two works, Kropotkin demonstrated that a scientific and efficient production process would render long working hours unnecessary. "If civilization and progress are to be compatible with equality, it is necessary that equality should not involve long hours of painful toil for little more than the necessaries of life, since where there is no leisure, art and science will die and all progress will become impossible."

The two major planks of Kropotkin's argument regarding work were that improvement in methods of production would make work more pleasant, and that the wage system should be abolished. To this end, he rejected any form of coercion or compulsion in human affairs, preferring instead consensus.

In *Anarchism* and *Anarchist Communism,* Kropotkin sketched anarchist principles with penetrating clarity:

> The anarchists consider, therefore, that to hand over to the state all the main sources of economical life—the land, the mines, the railways, banking, insurance, and so on—as also the management of all the main branches of industry, in addition to all the functions already accumulated in its hands (education, state-supported religions, defense of the territory, etc.) would mean to create a new instrument of tyranny. State capitalism would only increase the powers of bureaucracy and capitalism. True progress lies in the direction of decentralization, both territorial and functional, in the development of the spirit of local and personal initiative, and of free federation from the simple to the compound, in lieu of the present hierarchy from the center to the periphery.[33]

He was contemptuous of the state system and recommended its comprehensive abolition.

For Kropotkin, the ideal society was one in which the functions of government are reduced to the barest minimum, where "the individual recovers his full liberty of initiative and action for satisfying, by means of free groups and federations—freely constituted—all the infinitely varied needs of the human being."[34]

Since Kropotkin's time, many other writers have made significant contributions to anarchist theory, especially to the important task of outlining the possible forms that an anarchist society might take. One of the most important of these writers was Rudolf Rocker, whose most important works are *Anarchism and Anarcho-Syndicalism* and *Nationalism and Culture*. Contemporarily, Murray Bookchin has produced many valuable works, such as *Post-Scarcity Anarchism* and *Toward an Ecological Society*, and Graham Purchase's recent *Anarchism and Environmental Survival* is also worthy of note. It is beyond the scope of this chapter, however, to consider in depth the many possible forms an anarchist society might take.

For our purposes, suffice it to say that the foundation of anarchist *theory* lies in the rejection of coercion. The flip side—let us say the positive side—of this rejection is the belief in human freedom and equality as the highest good. From these premises, anarchists necessarily reject government (organized coercion and violence) and capitalism (organized economic domination of the individual), and instead embrace voluntary association, voluntary cooperation, persuasion, education, and mutual aid.

Anarchists recognize that means determine ends, and thus the means that anarchists embrace (voluntary association, cooperation, mutual aid, etc.) must necessarily be congruent with their ends. In the long run, this strategy will bear good fruit—a free and equal society; but in the short term this means that quick fixes are unlikely.

Like similar radical doctrines, anarchism derives in the main from humankind's relentless—if slow and tortured—quest for freedom, as well as from the desire for complete development of individuals through the release of their own initiatives and creative energies. This quest, ever-recurring in human society, is nothing new.

What distinguishes anarchism, as Bertrand Russell pointed out, is that the close relation of the anarchist ideal to human suffering has led to the birth of powerful social movements. It is this that makes anarchism "dangerous to those who batten, consciously or unconsciously, upon the evils of our present order of society."

The similarities and differences between anarchism and related ideological schools such as marxist socialism, syndicalism, and guild socialism are outlined in the next chapter.

---

1. *The New Encyclopaedia Britannica* (15th Edition), Volume I, 1990, p. 371.
2. *The Encyclopedia Americana* (International Edition), Volume I, 1981, p. 277.
3. *Collier's Encyclopedia*, Volume 2. New York: Macmillan, 1982, p. 127.
4. Russell, B. *Roads to Freedom*. London: Unwin, 1977, p. 44.
5. Ibid., p. 57.

6. Bakunin, M. *Marxism, Freedom and the State.* London: Freedom Press, 1984, p. 22.
7. Ibid., p. 5.
8. Ibid., p. 31.
9. Kropotkin, P. *Anarchism and Anarchist Communism.* London: Freedom Press, 1987, p. 23.
10. Ibid., p. 29.
11. Ibid., p. 51 and 52.
12. Bakunin, Op. Cit., p. 33.
13. Kropotkin, Op. Cit., p. 39.
14. Bakunin, Op. Cit., pp. 33 and 34.
15. Maximoff, G.P. *Program of Anarcho-Syndicalism.* Sydney: Monty Miller Press, 1985, p. 10.
16. Ibid., p. 11.
17. Ibid., p. 13.
18. See *The Principles, Aims and Statutes of the International Workers Association*
19. Dielo Trouda Group, *Organisational Platform of the Libertarian Communists,* 1926, Irish edition, republished by Workers Solidarity Movement, p. 18.
20. Maximoff, Op. Cit., p. 34.
21. See Doyle, K. *Workers Solidarity,* Issue #36, Autumn 1992, p. 20.
22. See *Statutes of the International Workers Association*
23. Anonymous, *You Can't Blow Up a Social Relationship: The Anarchist Case Against Terrorism.* Tucson, Arizona: See Sharp Press, 1990, p. 20.
24. Russell, Op. Cit., p. 56.
25. Quoted in Russell, Op. Cit., p. 57.
26. Bakunin, Op. Cit., p. 6.
27. See *Anarchism Toward the 21st Century,* published by Anarchist Media Institute, p. 27.
28. Kropotkin, Op. Cit., p. 11.
29. See Kropotkin, Op. Cit., p. 12.
30. Ibid.
31. See Bakunin, Op. Cit., pp. 12, 28, and 30. See also Russell, Op. Cit., pp. 48, 96 and 98.
32. Quoted in Russell, p. 51.
33. Kropotkin, Op. Cit., p. 9.
34. Ibid., pp. 23 and 2.

2

Anarchism In History

The relationship between anarchism and related social movements—notably syndicalism, guild socialism, and marxist socialism (in its 57 varieties: leninism, stalinism, maoism, trotskyism, social democracy, etc., etc.)—remains as contentious today as it ever was, even though they all share the common goal of the abolition of capitalism and the radical reconstruction of society.

Marxist socialism, of course, derives from the revolutionary writings of Karl Marx, who was inspired by the depressing spectacle of working-class misery in 19th-century industrial England. Many, including Bertrand Russell, credit Marx with producing the first coherent body of socialist doctrine.[1] It had three main planks: first, the materialist concept of history; second, the theory of the concentration of capital; and third, class war.

According to Marx's materialistic interpretation of history, the substructure, that is, the socioeconomic formation, provides the axis around which other aspects of society revolve. The substructure invariably determines the superstructure, namely social and political systems, and laws and values. However, the economic structure is not wholly determining; the economic, social, and ideological structures are interdependent and interact with one another in various ways, and mutually influence each other.

The theory of concentration of capital correctly anticipated the worldwide emergence of monopolies and oligopolies, spurred by the profit motive and including the export of capital, and culminating in the division of the world into a handful of usurer states and a multitude of debtor states.

Based on the foregoing, Marx conceived capitalists ("the bourgeoisie") and wage earners ("the proletariat") as being in perpetual conflict due to irreconcilably opposed economic interests. "The two classes, since they have antagonistic interests, are forced into a class-war which generates within the capitalist regime internal forces of disruption."[2]

As *The Communist Manifesto*[3] proclaims: "The history of all hitherto existing society is the history of class struggles." A resolution of the class war is possible only with the abolition of private ownership of the means of production, it says. Marx was to elaborate on these doctrines in detail in *Das Capital*, an immensely rigorous and technical critique of capitalism, as well as in a succession of brutally provocative works on capitalist production, distribution and exchange, and social relations.

Anarchism is, essentially, an outgrowth of the socialist movement. We believe that the historical connection between the world views of marxism and anarchism is as important as their marked differences. It is important, therefore, to return to the uneasy relationship that existed between Marx and Bakunin, and ultimately the convulsions within the first International Workingmen's Association.

Marx and Bakunin, by all accounts, did not get along well. Bakunin acknowledged Marx's genius and revolutionary zeal[4]; but at the same time he was quick to point out Marx's arrogance, egotism, and (German) nationalism. The following account is provided by Bakunin himself: "I respected him much for his learning and his passionate and serious devotion (always mixed, however, with personal vanity) to the cause of the proletariat, and I sought eagerly his conversation, which was always instructive and clever, when it was not inspired by paltry hate, which, alas! happened only too often. But there was never any frank intimacy between us. Our temperaments would not suffer it. He called me a sentimental idealist, and he was right; I called him a vain man, perfidious and crafty, and I also was right."[5]

This air of mutual antagonism persisted and permeated all facets of their relationship. It was profoundly evident in their involvement in the activities of the International Workingmen's Association after its founding in London in 1864. The First International had been founded largely by Marx as a platform for all workers and activists of socialist persuasion. The ideas of the First International "spread with remarkable rapidity in many countries and soon became a great power for the propagation of socialist ideas."[6]

Bakunin was not initially enthusiastic about the International, but that soon changed. While living in Italy in 1864, he founded the Alliance of Socialist Revolutionaries; and in 1869, in Switzerland, he co-founded the International Alliance of Socialist Democracy. The latter group applied to join the International, but its application was turned down because "branches must be local, and could not be international."[7] Members of the Alliance were subsequently admitted in sections after it had disbanded as a separate body in July 1869.

At the Fourth Congress of the International in Basel in September 1869, a major rift emerged between Marx and his followers on the one hand, and Bakunin and his followers on the other. Bakunin states that, "It was fundamentally a difference on the question as to the role of the state in the socialist programme. The Marxian view was essentially that the state must be used to bring about and consolidate socialism; the views of the Bakuninists (at this period beginning to be called anarchists) was that the state must be abolished, and that it could never under any circumstances be used to attain either socialism or any form of social justice for the workers."[8]

The Basel Congress, Bertrand Russell stated in a related account, gave birth to two strong currents within the International. "The Germans and English followed Marx in his belief in the state as it was to become after the abolition of private property; they followed him also in his desire to found labour parties in the various countries, and to utilise the machinery of democracy for the election of representatives of labour to parliaments. On the other hand, the Latin nations in the main followed Bakunin in opposing the state and disbelieving in the machinery of representative government."[9]

Dissension between these two camps deepened in intensity and scope both within the International and outside it. This culminated in the expulsion of Bakunin from the International at its General Congress in Amsterdam in 1872. There Bakunin had made a case for the International to be made a loose association of fully autonomous, national groups devoted only to the economic struggle as opposed to Marx's well known preference for a centralized political movement and all that goes with such a movement.

In the end, the International broke up, leaving in its wake two feuding factions embodying the fundamental differences between anarchism and marxist socialism—namely, total rejection of the state system by the former, and its embrace by the latter.

Engels had, in fact, advocated "a very strong government" within the overall framework of proletarian dictatorship to replace the capitalist state. Lucraft, a member of the General Council of the Basel Congress, had advanced the idea that all land in a country should become the property of the state, and that the cultivation of the land should be directed and administered by state officials, "which will only be possible in a democratic and socialist state, which the people will have to watch carefully over the good administration of the national land by the state."[10] Similarly, the German Social Democratic Labor Party, founded under the auspices of Marx, Bebel and Liebknecht, stated in its blueprint that the acquisition of political power was the preliminary condition for the economic emancipation of the proletariat. The state system was in this sense transitional, pending its withering away in the long term with the full accomplishment of the socialist revolution. At that point, all class differences and antagonisms would be eliminated, resulting in, as Engels put it, the "abolition of the state as a state." For marxist socialism, therefore, the withering away of the state constitutes an end in itself. Assuming that this were logical and feasible, it would still amount, in the transitional period, to fighting old tyrannies with new ones.

As Bakunin put it, "The Marxians think that, just as in the 18th century, the bourgeoisie dethroned the nobility to take its place and to absorb it slowly into its own body, sharing with it the domination and exploitation of the toilers in towns as well as in the country, so that the proletariat of the towns is called on today to dethrone the bourgeoisie, to absorb it, and to share with it the domination and exploitation of the proletariat of the countryside; . . ."[11] In other words, the marxists advocated not the abolition of coercive state power, but merely the substitution of a new dominator class for the old one at the helm of the state.

This mistake leads to others, such as advocacy of political parties and, in some varieties of marxism, participation in electoral politics as the primary means of attaining socialism. In his address to the General Congress of the International in Amsterdam in 1872, Marx stated: "We know that the institutions, customs and traditions of separate countries have to be taken into account; and we do not deny that there are countries like America and Britain . . . in which workers can achieve their goal by peaceful means."[12] By "peaceful means," of course, Marx meant electoralism and parliamentary action—simply put, political struggle which precludes tampering with the state system.

Even though both anarchism and marxist socialism have advocated the international solidarity of workers in all trades and in all countries in their economic struggle against the powers of capital, the issue of the state has constituted a major wedge between them.

Says Bakunin:

It is in the real organization of this solidarity, by the spontaneous organization of the working masses and by the absolutely free federation, powerful in proportion as it will be free, of the working masses of all languages and nations, and not in their unification by decrees and under the rod of any government whatever, that there resides the real and living unity of the International. . . . We do not understand that anyone could speak of international solidarity when they want to keep states . . . the state by its very nature being a rupture of this solidarity . . . State means domination and all domination presupposes the subjection of the masses, and consequently their exploitation to the profit of some minority or other.[13]

He adds in another passage:

The Marxists . . . console themselves with the idea that [their] rule will be temporary. They say that the only care and objective will be to educate and elevate the people economically and politically to such a degree that such a government will soon become unnecessary, and the State, after losing its political or coercive character, will automatically develop into a completely free organization of economic interests and communities.

There is a flagrant contradiction in this theory. If their state would really be of the people, why eliminate it? . . . Every state, not excepting their People's State, is a yoke, on the one hand giving rise to despotism and on the other to slavery. They say that such a yoke-dictatorship is a transitional step towards achieving full freedom for the people: anarchism or freedom is the aim, while state and dictatorship is the means, and so, in order to free the masses of the people, they have first to be enslaved!

Upon this contradiction our polemic has come to a halt. They insist that only dictatorship (of course their own) can create freedom for the people. We reply that all dictatorship has no objective other than self-perpetuation, and that slavery is all it can generate and instill in the people who suffer it. Freedom can be created only by freedom.[14]

As Bakunin foresaw, retention of the state system under socialism would lead to a barrack regime. Here the workers, peasants and the people as a whole "would wake, sleep, work and live to the beat of the drum; for the clever and the learned a privilege of governing."[15] Even if such a regime were democratically elected, it could still easily be a despotism. Bertrand Russell explains: "It is undeniable that the rule of a majority may be almost as hostile to freedom as the rule of a minority: the divine right of majorities is a dogma as little possessed of absolute truth as any other. A strong democratic state may easily be led into oppression of its best citizens, namely those whose independence of mind would make them a force for progress."[16]

Unfortunately, Bakunin's predictions about marxist socialism have proven to be uncannily accurate. Even some marxists have acknowledged this. One such acknowledgement came from Burton Hall in the Winter 1968 issue of *New Politics*:

> . . . it is most uncomfortable for a devout socialist to look over the argument exchanged between Marx and Bakunin and reflect that maybe it was Bakunin who was right all the time . . . not only because of the accuracy of his predictions as to what socialism would look like, if it were ever to come into existence, but even more to the point, because the reasoning on which he based these predictions, reinforced by the historical evidence of the past half-century, seems almost unanswerably persuasive.[17]

But having said that, it's still worthwhile to elucidate the parallels between anarchism and marxism. Conor McLoughlin outlines some of them: "Both systems were founded on the idea of historical materialism, both accepted the class struggle, both were socialist in the sense of being opposed to private property in the means of production. They differed in that Bakuninism refused to accept the state under any circumstances whatever, that it rejected politics or parliamentary action, and that it was founded on the principle of liberty as against that of authority."[18] McLoughlin concludes: "One can accept a materialist method of analysis and Marx's critique of capitalism without accepting the politics of Marx and Engels."

As well, marxism does not reject the anarchist program completely. Both anarchism and marxism champion the aspirations of the wage earner and seek the abolition of the wage system. Marxism, however, quarrels with the seeming impatience of anarchism as well as its willingness to ignore the "scientific" law of evolution which supposedly determines the orderly march of history. Both systems are nevertheless impelled by a common and genuine desire to extinguish the evils of capitalism through the abolition of wage labor, the ways and means of commodity exchange, and, most of all, the needless misery, inequality, and exploitation characterizing the relationship between the have-nots and the owners of capital.

There are similar striking parallels between anarchism, guild socialism, and syndicalism. An outlining of the latter two theories is thus necessary at this juncture.

Guild socialism, made popular through the writings of S.G. Hobson and G.D.H. Cole, strives toward autonomy in industry and a drastic curtailment in the powers of the state, but not its abolition. Put differently, for the workers' guild, the goal is not merely to secure better work conditions, but to achieve socialism through the control of industry. Each factory is to be free to manage its own affairs, including control of production through the supervision of managers elected directly by the workers. "The state would own the means of production as a trustee for the community: the Guilds would manage them, also as trustees for the community, and would pay to the state a single tax or rent. Any Guild that chose to set its own interests above those of the community would be violating its trust, and would have to bow to the judgement of a tribunal equally representing the whole body of producers and the whole body of consumers."[19]

This tribunal, known as the Joint Committee of Parliament and the Guild Congress, would adjudicate on matters involving the interests of consumers and producers alike. Below the joint committee lie two parallel bodies with equal powers: the parliament (state) representing the community in their capacity as consumers, and the guild congress, representing the community in their capacity as producers. Guild socialism postulates that all social systems to date have perceived society from the point of view of either producers or consumers, but never from both points of view. It thus insists on functional representation as a basis for the organization of society, which necessarily involves the abolition of the wage system. Its theoretical assumptions are summarized in the following:

Capitalism has made of work a purely commercial activity, a soulless and a joyless thing. But substitute the national service of the Guilds for the profiteering of the few; substitute responsible labour for a saleable commodity; substitute self-government and decentralization for the bureaucracy and demoralising hugeness of the modern state and the modern joint stock company; and then it may be just once more to speak of a "joy in labour" and once more to hope that men may be proud of quality and not only of quantity in their work.[20]

Syndicalism, on the other hand, is a social theory "which regards the trade union organisations as at once the foundation of the new society and the instrument whereby it is to be brought into being."[21] (The word "syndicalism" derives from the French words "syndicat" and "syndicalisme," which mean "trade union" and "trade unionism" respectively.) Syndicalism advocates direct action by the working class to abolish the capitalist order, including the state, and to establish in its place a social order based on workers organized in production units. The syndicalist movement, in concrete terms, grew out of a strong anarchist and anti-parliamentary tradition among the French working class, who were greatly influenced by the teachings of the anarchist P.J. Proudhon and the socialist Auguste Blanqui.

According to Bertrand Russell, "Syndicalism stands essentially for the point of view of the producer as opposed to that of the consumer, as it is concerned with reforming actual work and the organisation of industry, not merely with securing greater rewards for work."[22] In Appadori's words, "The syndicalists accept the general socialist position that society is divided into two classes, the capitalist and the proletariat, whose claims are irreconcilable; that the modern state is a class state dominated by the few capitalists; that the institution of private capital is the root of all social evils and that the only remedy for them is to substitute collective capital in place of private capital."[23]

The syndicalist current manifested itself within two French labor unions in the 1890s, the Confederation General du Travail (CGT—which declared revolutionary syndicalism its creed), and the Federation des Bourses du Travail (FBT), which led to their joining forces in 1902. The secretary general of the FBT, Fernand Pelloutier, himself essentially an anarchist, was influential in the formulation of syndicalist principles. "The task of the revolution is to free mankind, not only from all authority, but also from every institution which has not for its essential purpose the development of production,"[24] he stated.

Class war conducted by direct industrial methods at the point of production, including the general strike, the boycott, and sabotage (as opposed to electoral political methods) is held out as the principal syndicalist weapon. Being fundamentally opposed to capitalism, syndicalism advocates the abolition of the state: "The state was by nature a tool of capitalist oppression and, in any event, was inevitably rendered inefficient and despotic by its bureaucratic structure."[25]

Proceeding from this standpoint, syndicalists aim at using the strike as a means of undermining and eventually overthrowing capitalism, not simply as a means of securing better working conditions and wages. The ultimate expression of the strike as a weapon is the general strike (a total work stoppage in all services and industries), the aim of which is to paralyze the capitalist system.

Syndicalists are no less contemptuous of state socialism than anarchists, convinced that it is equivalent to state capitalism, with the state being the sole employer (with the police and army to back up its dictates); because of this, they are also convinced that the lot of the working class will be (and has been) even worse under state socialism than under corporate capitalism.

1. See Russell, B. *Roads to Freedom*. London: Unwin, 1977, p. 26.
2. Ibid., p. 29.
3. Quoted in Russell, p. 30.
4. For example, by 1869 he had begun a Russian translation of *Das Capital*, a book whose economic doctrine he enthusiastically supported.
5. Quoted in Russell, p. 48.
6. Ibid., p. 51.
7. Ibid.
8. Bakunin, M. *Marxism, Freedom and the State*. London: Freedom Press, 1984, pp. 11 and 12.
9. Russell, Op. Cit., p. 52.
10. Bakunin, Op. Cit., p. 39.
11. Ibid., p. 47.
12. Ibid., p. 43.
13. Ibid., p. 32.
14. Quoted in Dolgoff, S. (ed.) *Bakunin on Anarchy*. New York: Alfred A. Knopf, 1971, pp. 331-332.
15. Bakunin, Op. Cit., p. 16.
16. Russell, Op. Cit., p. 57.
17. Quoted in Dolgoff, Op. Cit., p. 323.
18. McLoughlin, C. "Anarchism and Marxism," *Workers Solidarity Magazine*, Issue #39, 1993.
19. Appadorai, A. *The Substance of Politics*. London: Oxford University Press, 1978, p. 124.
20. Ibid., p. 120.
21. See *The Encyclopaedia Britannica* (15th Edition), Vol. II, p. 464.
22. Russell, Op. Cit., p. 62.
23. Appadorai, Op. Cit., p. 120.
24. Quoted in *The New Radical Thinker*, Sept.–Dec. 1994. See also Russell, p. 64.
25. Russell, Op. Cit., pp. 65 and 66.

3

Anarchistic Precedents in Africa

Continental Africa covers about 11,500,000 square miles, running from the Mediterranean Sea to the Cape of Good Hope, and from the Western Bulge (Senegal) to the Eastern Horn (Somalia), together with the offshore islands of Cape Verde, Fernando Po, Madagascar, Mauritius, Zanzibar, the Comoros, and others.[1]

The territory that lies between the Sahara Desert and the tropical rain forest is the home of a variety of peoples. Between Senegal and Gambia live the Wolor and Tukulor, while between Gambia and the River Niger Valley live the Soninke, Mandigo, Khran, Tuareg, Ashanti, Banbara, and Djula. The Songhai dominate the middle Niger area, and the Masai inhabit the Upper Volta basin. Across the river in what is presently northwestern and north-central Nigeria live the Hausa-Fulani, while the Kanuri live in the northeast. Further south and spreading toward the east one finds the Igbo, Yoruba, Gikuyu, Luo, Shona, Ndebele, Xhosa, Bantu, Zulu, etc. To the north of the Sahara lies Egypt and the Maghredb region, which are peopled by African Arabs and Berbers.

To a greater or lesser extent, all of these traditional African societies manifested "anarchic elements" which, upon close examination, lend credence to the historical truism that governments have not always existed. They are but a recent phenomenon and are, therefore, not inevitable in human society. While some "anarchic" features of traditional African societies existed largely in past stages of development, some of them persist and remain pronounced to this day.

What this means is that the ideals underlying anarchism may not be so new in the African context. What is new is the concept of anarchism as a social movement or ideology. Anarchy as an abstraction may indeed be remote to Africans, but it is not at all unknown as a way of life. This is not fully appreciated because there is not as yet a systematic body of anarchist thought that is peculiarly African in origin. It is our intention in this chapter to unravel the manner and extent to which "anarchic elements" are indigenous to Africa and Africans.

AFRICAN COMMUNALISM

Traditional African societies were, for the most part, founded on *communalism*. The term is used here in two senses. First, it denotes a definite mode of production or social formation that comes generally, though not inevitably, after hunter-gatherer societies, and in turn precedes feudalism. If one accepts cultural evolution, one sees that most European and Asian societies passed through these stages of development.

Communalism is also used in a second, related sense to denote a way of life that is distinctly African. This way of life can be glimpsed in the collectivist structure of African societies in which: 1) different communities enjoy (near) unfettered independence from one another; 2) communities manage their own affairs and are for all practical purposes self-accounting and self-governing; and 3) every individual without exception takes part, either directly or indirectly, in the running of community affairs at all levels.

In contrast to Europe and Asia, most of Africa never developed past the stage of communalism. Despite the indigenous development of feudalism and the later imposition of capitalism, communal features persist to this day—sometimes pervasively—in the majority of African societies that lie outside the big cities and townships. Essentially, much of Africa is communal in both the cultural (production/social formation) and descriptive (structural) senses.

Among the most important features of African communalism are the absence of classes, that is, social stratification; the absence of exploitative or antagonistic social relations; the existence of equal access to land and other elements of production; equality at the level of distribution of social produce; and the fact that strong family and kinship ties form(ed) the basis of social life in African communal societies. Within this framework, each household was able to meet its own basic needs.[2] Under communalism, by virtue of being a member of a family or community, every African was (is) assured of sufficient land to meet his or her own needs.[3]

Because in traditional African societies the economy was largely horticultural and subsistence based, as Horton notes, "often small villages farmed, hunted, fished, etc., and looked after themselves independently with little reference to the rest of the continent." Various communities produced surpluses of given commodities which they exchanged, through barter, for those items that they lacked. The situation was such that no one starved while others stuffed themselves and threw away the excess.

According to Walter Rodney, "in that way, the salt industry of one locality would be stimulated, while the iron industry would be encouraged in another. In a coastal, lake or riverine area, dried fish could become profitable, while yams and millet would be grown in abundance elsewhere to provide a basis of exchange. . . ."[4] Thus, in many parts of Africa a symbiosis arose between groups earning their living in different manners—they exchanged goods and coexisted to their mutual advantage.

Political organization under communalism was horizontal in structure, characterized by a high level of diffusion of functions and power. Political leadership, not authority, prevailed, and leadership was not founded on imposition, coercion, or centralization; it arose out of a common consensus or a mutually felt need.

Leadership developed on the basis of family and kinship ties woven around the elders; it was conferred only by age, a factor which, as we shall see, runs deep in communalism. In Africa, old age was—and still often is—equated with possession of wisdom and rational judgment. Elders presided at meetings and at the settlement of disputes, but hardly in the sense of superiors; their position did not confer the far-reaching sociopolitical authority associated with the modern state system, or with feudal states.

There was a pronounced sense of equality among all members of the community. Leadership focused on the interests of the group rather than on authority over its members. Invariably, the elders shared work with the rest of the community and received more or less the same share or value of total social produce as everyone else, often through tribute/redistributive mechanisms.

The relationship between the coordinating segments of the community was characterized by equivalence and opposition, and this tended to hinder the emergence of role specialization, and thus the division of labor among individuals. Generally, elders presided over the administration of justice, the settlement of disputes, and the

organization of communal activities, functions they necessarily shared
with selected representatives of their communities, depending on the
specific nature of the dispute or issue involved.

Such meetings and gatherings were not guided by any known
written laws, for there were none. Instead, they were based on
traditional belief systems, mutual respect, and indigenous principles
of natural law and justice. Social sanctions existed for various kinds of
transgressions—theft, witchcraft, adultery, homicide, rape, etc. When
an individual committed an offense, often his entire household, his
kinsmen, and his extended family suffered with him, and sometimes
for him.[5] This was because such offenses were believed to bring shame
not only upon the individual, but even more so upon his relatives.

In traditional societies, Africans reached major decisions through
consensus, not by voting. What Nnamdi Azikiwe says of jurisprudence
in communal Nigeria is no less true of the rest of Africa:

> It is based on the concept of settlement of disputes by conciliation.
> It emphasises the need for amicable settlement of disputes by
> mutual compromise. . . . In its operation, the machinery of Nigerian
> justice shuns technicalities but places more emphasis on redress,
> impartiality, reasonableness and fair play . . . the positive legal
> system of Nigeria seeks to prevent the perpetuation of injustice and
> to enthrone equity, on the understanding that no person should be
> unjustly enriched or denied the elementary principles of natural
> justice.[6]

Likewise, religion held a cohesive role in African traditional society.
Individuals saw themselves as living in a world controlled by an
invisible order of personal beings of whom they had to take account
at every turn. "In such a world, the life of social groups, like other
things, is thought of as underpinned by spiritual forces."[7]

Religion, in this sense, was primarily "a theoretical interpretation
of the world, and an attempt to apply this interpretation to the
prediction and control of worldly events. Thus, there was always a
constant dialectic between religious ideas and principles of social
organisation and social form, and these, in turn, mutually reinforced
and influenced each other."[8]

The idea of "spiritual forces" translated into a notion of gods, an
earth spirit or a powerful guardian spirit that was personal to
individual members of the community. "A man's social field includes

not only relations with other men, but also relations with gods, and that the two kinds of relations have significant effects on one another. . . . In short, the gods are not only theoretical entities, they are people."[9] These ideas underpinned the existence of secret cults or secret societies in communal societies. As part of the political organization of communities, the roles of elders, age grades, and secret cults were not viewed as divine in this sense.

Among the social institutions that bound communities together were the age grades or age-set system. According to Azikiwe, "Usually, age grading divides adult males into elders and young adults—or more rarely into elders, middle-aged, and young adults. The age-grade system is usually fed by a system of age sets, whose members move from one grade to the next."[10] The rise of age grades was in itself a response to the need for greater communal solidarity, since age grades cut across families and lineages.

Age grades consisted of cohorts of males who came together to perform certain functions and duties. These included farm work for their members (or other members of society who asked for their services), road building, environmental sanitation, burials, and harvest of farm produce. A female equivalent of the age sets existed, although, as we shall see, their relative importance varied from society to society.

Secret societies—so called because their deliberations were kept secret from the public—performed ceremonial and religious functions, claiming to have links with the guardian spirit of the society. Secret societies also performed judicial functions, deciding the more intractable intra-village disputes. More importantly, it was the prerogative of secret societies to execute a community's decisions and resolutions. Admission into a secret society was open to adolescent males regardless of lineage.

Robert Horton unravels the mystique of secrecy that attends secret societies' deliberations and activities, which contrasts sharply with the "open free-for-all" of the age-grade system:

> This secrecy counters the influence of lineage rivalries in two ways. On the one hand, it protects those engaged in the deliberations against pressure from their various lineages. This makes it easier for them to consider any situation on its merits and to avoid taking up positions inspired by purely sectional interests. On the other hand, it enables the society to announce its decisions to the public as things collective and unanimous.[11]

Members of secret societies wore masks while executing the community's decisions, which often involved imposing sanctions on offenders. Horton further explains:

> This (wearing of masks) makes immediate sense when considered as a device to ensure acceptance of the harsher sanctions applied by the society to offenders. . . . Where the executives are masked, it is possible for the public to accept their actions, however harsh, as impersonal manifestations of the collective will. If they were unmasked and identifiable, their actions might cause dangerous resentment through suspicion of sectional interest.[12]

Collective action was the underlying social principle, and often there was collective responsibility and collective punishment of offenders.

Both the age grades and the secret societies performed quasi-military and police functions in the absence of a formal military institution, army, or police force. Every adult member of the community took an active part in the discharge of these functions for the good of the community, as a collectivity. Thus, for example, every adult male member of the community would be expected to participate in the search for a reported stolen or missing oxen, sheep, goat, or cow.

Increased production was achieved in communal African societies with the introduction of iron tools, notably the axe and hoe. According to Rodney, "It was on the basis of the iron tools that new skills were elaborated in agriculture as well as in other spheres of economic activity."[13]

No less instrumental to the achievement of increased production in the communal economy was the age grade system itself; members constituted a standing pool of labor in the service of the entire community.

Several sociopolitical changes in the communal economy accompanied the productive increases. The emergence of skilled iron workers created increasing specialization and division of labor, while increases in production opened up opportunities for trade, profiteering, and the accumulation of disproportionate wealth in a few hands. With expanded trading activities, barter began to give way to the use of metallic objects as standards for valuing other goods.

An immediate fallout of these changes was the gradual breakdown of certain features of communalism and the rise of social stratification, albeit at a very low level. By the turn of the 15th century, several African societies were undergoing a transition from communalism to a class system. Social stratification formed the basis for the eventual rise of classes and the development of antagonistic social relationships, culminating in the establishment of empire states with centralized forms of government in some parts of Africa.

It must be emphasized that, on the whole, although slavery existed in different parts of Africa, especially in areas with the greatest erosion of communal equality, African society never really witnessed an epoch of slavery as a mode of production. Feudalism did exist in some places, but as Rodney has demonstrated, "in Africa, there is no doubt that the societies which eventually reached feudalism were extremely few." Consequently, some features of communalism continued to hold considerable sway in most African societies, as they do to this day under modern capitalist states. This demonstrates the ancient and tenacious roots of the communal way of life in Africa. At the least, Robert Horton observes, a society that has once known and enjoyed the conveniences of genealogical reckoning does not lightly drop them.

The manifestations of "anarchic elements" in African communalism, as we have seen above, were (and to some degree still are) pervasive. These include the palpable absence of hierarchical structures, governmental apparatuses, and the commodification of labor. To put this in positive terms, communal societies were (and are) largely self-managing, equalitarian and republican in nature.

Despite the marked equality and egalitarianism generally associated with African communalism, there existed a degree of privilege and internal differentiation in some communities, made worse sometimes by the traditional caste system. In addition, the high degree of egalitarianism and freedom achieved under communalism was made possible in no small measure by low levels of production.

So, communalism was not an anarchist utopia. Nowhere is this more evident than in the generally low status of women in some forms of communalism. This was made worse, at least on the surface, by the practice of polygyny (one man married to several women, often sisters). In many African communities, however, tradition and custom accorded certain protections to females; most injuries to them—with the important exceptions of clitoridectomy and infibulation in some societies—were severely punished. And there were some matrifocal communal societies, famous for their tradition of women leaders.

According to Samir Amin, prior to the emergence of empire states in Africa there existed a "village mode of production" which is comparable to Marx's category of primitive communism. This village mode of production, he says, was characterized by a limited geographical area and was carried on without a central expropriating body, namely the state. Thus, there was no external agency regulating the productive processes.

Similarly, ownership of the means of production was collective, just as social produce was universally consumed. Social surplus was low, and, as Bede Onimode explains, what surplus there was got used up in the reciprocity of gift-giving, which contributed to social cohesion. As the main productive unit of society, each family controlled the use of its own surplus produce. The breakdown of communalism in its pure, undiluted form, and the transition to semi-feudalism in certain parts of Africa, did not substantially alter these facts.

STATELESS SOCIETIES IN AFRICA

Some historians and scholars have distinguished between two broad groups in pre-colonial Africa: communities that established empire states and those that did not. Anthropologist Paul Bohannan refers to Africa's stateless societies as "tribes without rulers," a form of "ordered anarchy."[14]

Elsewhere, Rodney describes stateless communities as:

Those peoples who had no machinery of government coercion and no concept of a political unit wider than the family or the village. After all, if there is no class stratification in a society, it follows that there is no state because the state arose as an instrument to be used by a particular class to control the rest of society in its own interests . . . One can consider the stateless societies as among the older forms of sociopolitical organization in Africa, while the large states represented an evolution away from communalism—sometimes to the point of feudalism.[15]

The term "stateless societies" has been used in a pejorative sense by certain European scholars to denote backwardness arising from the inability of African societies to establish their own states. State formation in Africa, says the "Hamitic theory," was attributable to foreign influence, the belief being that Africans left on their own would never have been able to produce anything more than a "low" level of political organization. Among the stateless societies that existed on the continent were the Igbo, the Birom, Angas, Idoma, Ekoi, Nbembe, the Niger Delta peoples, the Tiv (Nigeria), the Shona (Zimbabwe), Lodogea, the Lowihi, the Bobo, the Dogon, the Konkomba, the Birifor (Burkina Faso, Niger), the Bate, the Kissi, the Dan, the Logoli, the Gagu and Kru peoples, the Mano, Bassa Grebo and Kwanko (Ivory Coast, Guinea, Togo), the Tallensi, Mamprusi, Kusaasi (Ghana), the Nuer (Southern Sudan), etc.—numbering today nearly two hundred million individuals in all.

For the purposes of a clear and retrospective understanding of stateless societies, we shall present case studies of three of them: the Igbo, the Niger Delta people (in present-day Nigeria), and the Tallensi (Ghana). Stateless societies tended generally to be agricultural, sedentary, and homogenous in character.

THE IGBO

Oral tradition has it that the ancestors of Igbos (also referred to as the Ibo) originated from somewhere in the Middle East. The earliest settlements of the Igbos were at Awka and Orlu, from which they spread south, pushing the Ibibios to the coastal fringes of the Niger Delta. The Igbo generally followed a segmentary pattern of political and social organization. As against large, centralized political units, Igbo society constructed small units, often referred to as "village" political units without kings or chiefs ruling over them or administering their affairs. "In Igbo, each person hails . . . from the particular district where he was born, but when away from home all are Igbos."[16] Among the Igbo, there is a popular saying, "*Igbo enwegh Eze*," meaning Igbo have no kings.

The smallest unit in the segmentary political system was the extended family with a common lineage; several extended families constituted a ward; and many wards formed a village. The affairs of a village community were controlled by four major institutions: the general assembly of all citizens, the council of elders, the age grades, and the secret societies, that acted as instruments of social control.

There was also the *Umu-ada,* a parallel body of women either married into the village or born there. The Umu-ada played a key role in decision making and implementation processes, as well as in maintaining the social values of the society. It was impossible, for instance, to make a decision on an issue that directly affected women or children without the consent of the Umu-ada.

Members of the council of elders were usually heads of extended families and were sometimes required to perform priestly functions. To this day, general assemblies of all citizens are a common feature of Igbo society. It is the duty of the town crier, wielding his gong, to go around the village in the evening after villagers have returned from their farms to summon everyone to the village square at a specified time. The purpose of the assembly is often tersely stated. At the village square, elders outline an issue in detail and the people are expected to air their views as forthrightly as possible, until a consensus is achieved. Neither the elders, the secret societies, nor the age grades could drag the village into a war or armed conflict without first consulting a general assembly for a decision.[17] The small scale of Igbo social institutions made true democracy possible. According to historian Isichei, "one of the things that struck the first Western visitors to Ibgoland was the extent to which democracy was truly practiced. An early visitor to a Niger Igbo town said that he felt he was in a free land, among a free people."[18] Another visitor, a Frenchman, said that true liberty existed in Igboland, though its name was not inscribed on any monument.[19]

Despite the segmentary lineage system of the Igbo, there existed links which brought several groups together as one people. Chief among these links were marriage and trade. [West Africa in general is known for its tradition of women traders—Ed.] Igbo custom and tradition encouraged inter-village marriage. Of the greatest importance in forging bonds of unity among the Igbo were the oracles, who served to bring them together to common shrines.

Being forest-dwelling people, Igbos grew enough food to feed themselves, using communal labor provided by both the age grade and extended family systems. Igbo social organization, like that of the Niger Delta people, Tiv, and Tallensi, manifested a definite inclination toward leadership as opposed to authority. Yet there were a few exceptions in Igboland, like the Onitsha and Nri communities, that had their own chiefs.

THE NIGER DELTA PEOPLES

The peoples of the Niger Delta can be divided into Ibibios, Ijaws, Urhobos, etc. Slave trade was rife in this area in the 17th and 18th centuries. The people were mostly traders and farmers. The basis of political cum social organization in this area was very small units, referred to as the "house" system, complete with extended families, age grades and secret societies. The latter played an important role among the Ibibios particularly, where control of political institutions was in the hands of members of the secret societies rather than lineage groups, as was the case in Igboland.[20]

A "house" consisted of a farmer or trader, his slaves, his own descendants, and those of his slaves. A number of "houses" comprised a city-state. Inter-house disputes were settled by a city assembly made up of house chiefs and presided over by an elected chief.

The Ijaws were divided into four main clans or city-states: Nembe, Kalabari, Brass, and Warri. The town assembly was responsible for communal policy making. The "Sakapu" secret society exercised both administrative and judicial functions. The mode of organization of the Urhobos was similar to that of the Ijaws in all respects. However, one group in the Niger Delta, the Itsekiri, had a centralized kinship pattern of government, similar to those of the Bini and the Yoruba.

As time went on, in certain areas the house system changed. With increased involvement in the booming overseas slave trade and later in legitimate trade, the house system, previously organized on the basis of lineage groups, was replaced by what was known as the "canoe house system." Under this system, people from different lineage groups combined to form a corporation for the purpose of trade.

THE TALLENSI

The Tallensi occupy the northern territories of the old Gold Coast (now Ghana). Today, they are peasant farmers, engaged mainly in the cultivation of cereal crops. The essential feature of their traditional agriculture is mixed farming, involving permanent and stable settlements, which profoundly influenced the social organization which was based on the clan system.

Clusters of homesteads were known as "suman." A residential aggregate constituted a clan, or a group of clans, members of which were kinfolk by consanguinity. Rights and duties, privileges and obligations were vested in corporate units, and any authorized member could act on behalf of the unit or clan. Each lineage was headed by a senior male member, who together with other clan elders constituted a repository of social and ritual responsibilities. Both the age grade system and the practice of convening mass assemblies to make crucial decisions were prevalent among the Tallensi. Groups and not individuals constituted the source of political authority.[21]

The various clans depended, for the most part, on communal labor. It was possible for large lineages within clans to accumulate wealth based on their size; however, no social privileges attached to wealth. Socially and politically, therefore, the Tallensi were a homogenous, sedentary and egalitarian society.

*   *   *

What is immediately prominent in our consideration of stateless societies is the absence of centralization and concentration of authority. For the most part it is difficult to point to any individual as the overall head or ruler of different communities. The exercise of leadership in the sense of full-time authority was similarly unknown. Whatever authority that existed often affected very limited aspects of the lives of individuals. At the same time, classes hardly existed in these traditional societies. It is indeed doubtful whether an equivalent for the word "class" exists in any indigenous African language—and language reflects the thoughts and values of those who speak it.

Increased productivity and specialization in the use of tools, together with increased trading activities between various communities on the one hand, and with outsiders on the other, gave rise to a steady growth of private property, internal differentiation/stratification, and semi-feudalism. Warfare, conquest, and voluntary borrowing were some of the other factors at work during the period of colonial transition.

Early authority patterns were commonly codified in ritualized forms of leadership. Even where systems of social control increased in scope, ritual leaders in many cases continued to exert a moderating influence over secular leaders. Empire states were established at Kanem-Bornu, Songhai, Mali, Oyo, Sokoto, Benin, Zulu, Ngwato, Memba, Bayankole, Kede, Somuke, Hausa-Fulani, etc.

COLONIALISM AND THE INCORPORATION OF AFRICA
INTO THE WORLD CAPITALIST ECONOMY

Africa's incorporation into the world capitalist economy was preceded by the systematic penetration of capitalist influences into the continent prior to colonialism. But colonialism accelerated and solidified the incorporation process.[22]

Capitalist influences first made themselves felt in Africa during the quest for economic expansion that accompanied and followed the industrial revolution in Europe. One of the first and most important of these influences was the slave trade. Capitalist penetration further increased through mercantilist activities and the operations of foreign businesses in African coastal areas toward the end of the 19th century.[23]

It should be emphasized that the process of penetration and the subsequent incorporation of the different African societies into the world capitalist economy was not an even one, and did not take place simultaneously all over the continent. In the Muslim societies, Islam was an important feature of the incorporation process, as well as a source of resistance to it. On the one hand, Islam provided a source of inspiration for resistance, while on the other it provided a basis for class collaboration between Muslim aristocrats and colonial administrators.[24]

All over Africa, the new gospel of free trade provided the ideological basis for the expansion of British, German, and French trading in the coastal areas. Following the Berlin Conference of 1884-1885, a violent scramble for the partition of Africa ensued among the major European powers, marking the beginning of true colonial domination and the enthronement of imperial interests over those of traditional societies. The imposition of colonial governments was an expression of this domination, and economic motives, primarily the quest for markets and raw materials, constituted its raison d'etre.

There were two stages in the process of incorporation, in which the state served as a vehicle for capitalist penetration and ultimate engulfment of production and distribution in the colonies. The first stage was violent conquest, and the next was economic domination and enslavement of the native peoples.[25] Forced labor was prominent among the mechanisms adopted by the colonial powers to eliminate traditional economic organization.

In addition to military actions, conquest involved the forceful ejection of natives from their lands, which were then seized by the colonialists. And this seizure was protected through the violent suppression of all forms of dissent by the coercive apparatus of the colonial state.

The period of conquest was followed by the introduction of new production processes. The fundamental objective of this restructuring was to bind the incorporated economies into the world economy. The critical weapons here were monetarization (the introduction of money), trade, wage labor, taxation, and investment, coupled with the development of appropriate social institutions and infrastructure. This always involved the introduction of incentives aimed at dissuading the local populace from investing in areas of local need, and instead to turn to production of cash crops and related goods and services.

It was primarily to this end that a monetary system was introduced. By a monetary system, we refer to the use of money (that is, inherently nonvaluable objects or tokens) not only as a medium of exchange, but, more importantly, to the elevation of money and its accoutrements to a level of cultural preponderance within both the economy and society as a whole. Money is, after all, *the* basic prerequisite of a market economy, without which exchange and economic growth are impossible. The process of monetarization thus went hand in hand with the spread of capitalist relations of production.[26]

As noted earlier, a capitalist economy requires the establishment of social and political institutions that reproduce and regulate class relations. The colonial education system served such a purpose. Together with the church, another agent of socialization, it provided ideological justification for the emergent capitalist mode of production in Africa. As well, it's worth noting that there was no clear cut distinction between the state and the church on the one hand, and the church and the school on the other—they formed an integrated system of ideological support for colonialism/capitalism. Indeed, colonial education was a common basis for class alliance between colonialists and local bureaucrats. Political parliamentarianism was the inevitable result of such education.

Overall, the process of Africa's incorporation into the world capitalist network started during the latter stages of communalism, lasted through feudalism, and continues to the present day in the form of neocolonialism.

THE IMPACT OF INCORPORATION

The ultimate result of Africa's incorporation into the world capitalist economy was the destruction of the traditional pre-colonial communal mode of production. As the capitalist mode developed, it confronted the noncapitalist mode, violently transforming various communities, turning their lands, resources, and products into commodities. Countless thousands of able-bodied young men were uprooted from their homes to work in capitalist enterprises, and the remaining population was compelled to grow only those crops that possessed exchange value—cash crops.

The critical point here is that the destruction of the traditional economic system did not give rise to a fully capitalist economy; the end product was, rather, a distorted, unbalanced capitalist structure. This occurred because Africa's incorporation into the global system was peripheral. Complementarity and reciprocity between the various sectors of the economy were absent. Misarticulation was further characterized by a lack of vital linkages within the production process. That is, capitalist development in Africa was characterized by lack of integration. Under colonialism, businesses operated to serve external markets, and usually had little connection with each other; and businesses that would have served internal needs were often systematically discouraged in order to ensure markets for goods produced in the imperial countries. Africa is still suffering the effects of that distorted development pattern.

So, capitalist penetration and subsequent integration of African societies into the global system has generated a culture of dependence —a dependence of the periphery (Africa) on the center (the advanced capitalist countries). Profits and surplus value are constantly being transferred from the periphery to the center. Conversely, economic and social crises in the global capitalist chain are readily transmitted to its weakest links—the highly susceptible periphery. As for the "development" of Africa by the West, Leonard Goncharov notes: "Capital is being exported from the highly developed capitalist countries to the developing countries, not actually with the aim of providing aid to the latter, but with the express purpose of deriving the highest possible profit."[27]

Finally, Africa's participation in the global capitalist economy has led to the creation of a local privileged class that appropriates surplus social produce, because capitalism cannot function without the existence of an exploitative, nay parasitic, local class. However, since the indigenous privileged played only a minor role in laying the basic foundations of the post-colonial state, its interests are subordinated to those of the foreign capitalists, primarily multinational corporations. As a result, a class alliance developed between the two, with the indigenous class assuming the role of agents for international capital. Its members live on the commissions they receive as middlemen. The dominance of this social class, coupled with the absence of autonomy in Africa's role in the world economy, has essentially transformed African states into fiefdoms.

CLASS FORMATION IN POST-COLONIAL AFRICA

To understand the dynamics of class formation in post-colonial Africa, we need first to examine the character of the preceding colonial state. Colonialism left independent African states with a neo-colonial economy, with the capitalist mode of production replacing the pre-capitalist modes; this entailed the subjugation of local labor and resources to the needs of capitalism.[28]

The classes that developed after this integration do not reflect an autonomous economy, but a dependent economy—they show an artificial and truncated version of the class structure of the developed Western economies. This class structure is not the classical division into capitalist class, petit bourgeoisie, working class and/or peasantry, but rather a simplified division into an administrative class and working class/peasantry. That is, classes in the former colonies are composed simply of those who benefit from neo-colonialism and those who suffer from it.

The local business class effectively became a comprador class of agents, middlemen, and front men for foreign interests. As Franz Fanon put it, the national bourgeoisie of underdeveloped societies is not engaged in production or any creative enterprise, but in intermediary activities. The roles of the local and foreign business classes in post-colonial Africa are complementary, but the latter determine the activities of the former.

The quest to create indigenous industry by African capitalists gives them a nationalist image, but they stop short at the demand for expropriation of foreign capital, upon which they remain dependent. The nationalism of this indigenous capitalist class is the outcome of its desire to appropriate resources (at least for itself) back from the foreign expropriator; and at the same time its commitment to freedom for foreign capital is necessitated, indeed dictated, by its dependence on neo-colonial economic structures. In any event, the conflicts of interest between indigenous capitalists and foreign capitalists often resolve themselves in accommodations that border on delineation of spheres of influence.[29]

Contrary to the local capitalists' pretensions to autonomy, foreign capital still holds the key to local economies through control of technology, finances, location of research and development facilities, appointment of technical directors, and, in general, control of decision making.

For example, a typical industrial investment in Africa depends on capital-intensive technology developed to meet the needs of advanced capitalist economies. This facilitates the outflow of resources as profits and payments for imports and services, and ties the investment to the producers of its technology. This, of course, places a considerable drain on scarce foreign exchange resources.

This pattern of investment generates and depends upon an inegalitarian pattern of income distribution. In turn, inegalitarian income distribution creates far more benefits for advanced capitalist economies than for neo-colonies.[30]

The dependent character of the local bourgeoisie restricts its members to servicing foreign capital or to competing among themselves for the limited resources available in the neo-colonial setting. This competition tends to take the form of a zero-sum game, modified by an arrangement in which the competitors define themselves in ethnic and religious terms—each seeking to protect his own interests.

The crux of our analysis is that the process of class formation in post-colonial Africa looks haphazard and incomplete: it took place only in the commercial and distributive sectors of the various economies, while the agricultural and industrial sectors were left out. This should, however, be understood within the following context: while the comprador class is the foremost beneficiary of Africa's neo-colonial political economy, various other segments of the local capitalist class also benefit through bureaucratic structures which entitle them to privileges.[31]

AFRICAN SOCIALISM

The global socialist current did not pass Africa by. For the most part, socialist ideas inspired national liberation struggles and permeated the ranks of the anti-colonial struggle—not least of all in the African trade union movement, dating back to the 1940s. The main attraction of socialism at that point was its sloganeering appeal. The prime movers of the anti-colonial struggle had neither a firm grasp of the socialist world view, nor the foggiest mental construct of what a socialist society would look like in the aftermath of the abolition or overthrow of capitalism. This shallow, confused concept of socialism—and the circumstances under which socialist ideas first came to Africa—would later have a decidedly negative impact on the growth and development of the socialist movement in Africa.

The dawn of political independence in the different African states forced the indigenous, nominally socialist political class to come to terms with the daunting task of trying to construct socialism on the continent. The leading lights of the movement in this period were Kwame Nkrumah (Ghana), Sekou Toure (Guinea), Patrice Lumumba (Congo), Tom Mboya and Jomo Kenyatta (Kenya), Sedar Senghor (Senegal), Modibo Keita (Mali), and Julius Nyerere (Tanzania).

This crop of leaders would later be joined in their romantic socialism by a second generation of political actors, including Muammar Gadhafi (Libya), Gamel Abdel Nasser (Egypt), Augustino Neto (Angola), and others, who, like the first generation leaders, almost invariably proclaimed their respective countries socialist and proceed to institute "socialism" as a matter of state policy.

Common to all these figures was the notion of an "African socialism," a unique brand of socialism peculiarly suited to the African in his own environment. It ranged from Nkrumah's positive socialism to Senghor's existential and "negritude" socialism, to Nasser's democratic socialism, to Nyerere's Ujamaa socialism.

Nkrumah proclaimed the goals of positive socialism as full employment, good housing, equal opportunities for education, and the cultural advancement of all people. In his theory of consciencism, Nkrumah states: "Revolutions are brought about by men . . . who think as men of action and act as men of thought."[32]

Senghor saw socialism as essentially a new vision of the world:

Such is the African way, at least, the Senegalese way to socialism. It intends to be a harmonic democracy, in both the political and economico-social fields. Far from rejecting them, it integrates European contributions. But it is quite a different matter from mere repetition, from a policy of blind imitation. These contributions selected with care, shall be integrated into and impregnated by the values of negritude. For negritude is nothing else but the whole of the living values of black Africa.[33]

For his part, Nasser characterized socialism as "the assertion of the sovereignty of the people and the placing of all authority in their hands and the consecration of all powers to serve their ends—the setting up of a society on a basis of sufficiency and justice, of work and equal opportunity for all, and of production and services." He advocated a two-stage revolution: a political revolution that enables the people to recover their right to self-government, and a social revolution—a class conflict that terminates ultimately in the realization of social justice for all.

African socialism, for what it's worth, has been variously criticized for lacking theoretical coherence and clarity, and, worse still, for the questionable manner in which it seeks to isolate world socialism from that practiced in Africa. Critics of African socialism have pointed out that exploitation and oppression are universal evils, and that socialism is universal in scope and application (though it can be adapted to suit individual cultures).[34] It's also worth noting that all of the varieties of African Socialism were state-socialist varieties, and they thus suffered the typical defects of state socialism wherever it appears; however, largely because of lack of a fully developed party/coercive apparatus, at least a few African "socialist" countries were spared the worst excesses of state socialism.

The balance sheets of the different socialist states and the various regimes that came to power bespeak lack of achievement, and the same, sometimes even worse, authoritarian inclinations that characterized the erstwhile colonial states and colonial masters. All of the reactionary germs of marxist state socialism present in the Soviet Union, Eastern Europe, North Korea, China and Cuba were present in African state socialism, even in its most primitive stages. And, uniquely, African state socialism elevated ethnic (tribal) and religious sentiments to the level of state ideology.

Despite socialist rhetoric, capitalist relations of production remained dominant for the most part in "African socialist" societies. Corruption and primitive accumulation through use of state powers and resources characterized the dominant political class. Labor repression was pronounced; in fact, the earlier lot of the worker under colonial and post-colonial capitalism often was better than under the very underdeveloped state socialist structures spawned by self-serving "socialists" and, sometimes, gun-toting soldiers and military officers as well.

Socialism in Africa, for all practical purposes, was based on the Soviet/Eastern European model, and it displayed all the essential features and characteristics of that model. The African experience was, perhaps, peculiar in the sense that the state inherited at political independence was neo-colonial. Expectations that socialism would alter this were never realized; if anything, socialism truncated development and reinforced neo-colonialism. The pauperization of countries like Guinea under Sekou Toure, Benin under Mathew Kerekou, Ethiopia under Menghistu Mariam, etc., went hand in hand with massive repression and authoritarian self-righteousness. Some of the most backward, most reactionary regimes that ever set foot on African soil were socialist ones, some led by military officers who shot their way to power.

There are many examples of failed socialist states in Africa, the worst probably being Menghistu's Ethiopia; others include Gadhafi's Libya, Kerekou's Benin, and Sekou Toure's Guinea. Nkrumah in Ghana and Bourmedine in Algeria made the most thorough, far-reaching attempts to install socialism in Africa; and both failed. The sole seeming exception to this string of failures is the genuine and credible attempt made in Tanzania under Nyerere to build socialism using the Ujamaa village scheme as a springboard. (It failed all the same, as we shall see.)

We can safely say that long before communism collapsed in the Soviet Union and Eastern Europe, socialism had failed in Africa, provoking in its wake interminable crises and turmoil. The overthrow of Nkrumah in Ghana and the exit of Nasser in Egypt, coupled with the failure of the Ujamaa program in Tanzania, and the popular uprising against Algerian state socialism are symptomatic of this failure.

IS THERE AN AFRICAN ANARCHISM?

Is there a developed, systematic body of thought on anarchism that is of African origin? Because anarchism as a way of life is in large measure indigenous in Africa, it seems almost certain that Africans had, at one time or another, formulated creative ideas on this way of organizing society. But any such ideas were almost certainly never recorded in written form. It is not surprising then, that many ideas were not preserved.[35] Much of the existing literature on African communalism and traditional African societies is based on the latter day works and writings of European anthropologists, historians, archaeologists, sociologists and, more recently, their African counterparts. Nonetheless, these works and the ideas in them are fragmented and disjointed with regard to anarchist concepts and principles.

The different strands of advanced, nonacademic African thought—from the time of colonial rule to the post-independence period—on the matters of socialism, revolution, and colonialism, are not so fragmented. For instance, in the euphoria that attended Nigeria's independence in 1960, both the Eastern and Western regional governments enunciated a program of farm settlements designed, among other things, to: a) extend the frontiers of freedom and initiative which the average farmer brought to bear on his work; b) free farming and agricultural production from drudgery; and c) lay the foundation for the emergence of agro-allied, medium-scale industries.[36]

The program, a pet idea of the radical, left-leaning faction of Nigeria's emergent local ruling class—for whom independence meant more than an opportunity for self-government—was modeled on the popular Israeli Kibbutz system and was intended to recreate the traditional African communal way of living, complete with its features of equality and freedom. Under the arrangement, farmers lived with their families in collectives and shared in common the means of production, including farming tools and implements, as well as utilities and infrastructure. Social produce was distributed equally among the farmers and their families, and the surplus was exchanged through the farmers' cooperatives.

The settlements were intended to be self-managing and self-accounting. Local communities provided land, while the government granted the farmers credit, and allocated the land to individual farmers or groups of farmers. The ultimate decision regarding what to plant lay with the farmer or group.

Scattered in selected villages and communities, the settlements were efficient and made tremendous increases in production, while they lasted. Soon, however, the egalitarian principles that informed the original program were eroded through bureaucratic bottlenecks and corruption; and the outbreak of the Nigerian civil war in 1967 finally spelled the collapse of the experiment.

Similar anarchic elements are discernible to a lesser degree in Muammar Gadhafi's famous "Green Book," which contains the so-called Third Universal Theory. The concept of *jamarrhiriyah*—people's collectives rooted in the countryside, making decisions in all matters concerning themselves—seems quite fascinating on paper. In practice, the proposals that Ghadafi set out were generally followed more in the breach than in practice.

Franz Fanon's unprecedentedly brutal critique of colonialism in Africa also contains grains of anarchist principles which are, unfortunately, sometimes obscured by anti-colonial rhetoric and rage. The full extent of Fanon's anger comes out when he dwells on the racial aspects of colonialism. Fanon's pillory of colonialism is at the same time a rejection of corporate capitalism. He advocates revolutionary class war, which is implicit in his two-part theory of violence and spontaneity.[37] Fanon repudiates those who deny that colonial powers derive material benefits from colonialism. His argument anticipates the basic thesis of contemporary underdevelopment theorists that, like capitalism, colonialism was rapacious, exploitative, and above all had precluded colonized societies' autonomous development.

Fanon's analysis marked something of a break with classical marxist theory. Although Marx and Engels indicted the moral basis of colonialism and regarded it as "activated by vilest interests," they nevertheless saw redeeming features in colonial rule as the unconscious tool of history in bringing about revolution.[38]

If, as Marx and Engels seem to be arguing, colonialism provided material benefits to the colonized, Fanon would counter that such benefits were inconsequential compared to the abject poverty and weak material position of colonized societies. Colonialism proved incapable of releasing and generating productive forces that Marx and

Engels had hoped would destroy the "Asiatic mode of production." Fanon argues that colonialism, like capitalism, was preceded, inaugurated, and maintained by violence, and could only be overthrown through the spontaneous action of revolutionary armed struggle.[39]

Fanon placed responsibility for waging armed struggle not on political parties, trade unions, and urban working classes, but on the masses of all the people, from the peasantry in the countryside to the "lumpen proletariat," who, in his words, formed the political class often dismissed by marxists as "adventurers and anarchists."

His tersely articulated vision of the post-colonial period runs thus:

> When the people have taken violent part in the national liberation, they will allow no one to set themselves up as "liberators." They show themselves to be jealous of the results of their action, and take good care not to place their future, their destiny or the fate of their country in the hands of a living god . . . Illuminated by violence, the consciousness of the people rebels against any pacification. From now on, the demagoguery of the opportunists and the magicians has a difficult task. The action which has thrown them into a hand-to-hand struggle confers upon the masses a voracious taste for the concrete. The attempt at mystification becomes, in the long run, practically impossible.[40]

*　　*　　*

It is ultimately in the seminal thoughts of Julius Nyerere that we glean an organized, systematic body of doctrine on socialism that is indisputably anarchistic in its logic and content. Nyerere's notion of socialism revolves around the concept of *Ujamaa*, his pet program of "villagization"—where the village is billed as an incubator, a nursery of the socialism of the future. Ujamaa, which simply translates as "familyhood," represents rural economic and social communities where people live and work together for the good of all; their governments are chosen and led by the peasants and workers themselves.

Nyerere's concept of Ujamaa was predicated on the simplicity, egalitarianism and freedom that were the hallmarks of traditional African societies.[41] For instance, the organization of communal societies, especially the production and distribution of social produce, was such that there was hardly any room for parasitism:

In traditional African society, everybody was a worker. There was no other way of earning a living for the community. Even the elder, who appeared to be enjoying himself without doing any work . . . had, in fact, worked hard all his younger days. . . . In our traditional African society, we were individuals within a community. We took care of the community and the community took care of us. We neither needed nor wished to exploit our fellow men . . . every member of the family had to have enough to eat, some simple covering, and a place to sleep, before any of them (even the head of the family) had anything extra.[42]

He explains the concept of African land tenure thusly:

To us in Africa, land was always recognized as belonging to the community. Each individual within our society had a right to the use of land, because otherwise he could not earn his living, and one cannot have the right to life without also having the right to some means of maintaining life. But the African's right to land was simply the right to use it: he had no other right to it, nor did it occur to him to try and claim one.[43]

Nyerere contrasts the foregoing with capitalist society, which fails to give its citizens the means to work, or having given them the means to work, prevents them from getting a fair share of the products of their toil. "Ujamaa . . . is opposed to capitalism, which seeks to build a happy society on the basis of the exploitation of man by man; and it is equally opposed to doctrinaire socialism."[44] Under Ujamaa basic goods were to be held in common and shared among all members of the unit.

There was an acceptance that whatever one person had in the way of basic necessaries, they all had; no one could go hungry while others hoarded food and no one could be denied shelter if others had space to spare . . . a society in which all members have equal rights and equal opportunities; in which all can live at peace with their neighbors without suffering or imposing injustice, being exploited or exploiting; and in which all have a gradually increasing basic level of material welfare before any individual lives in luxury.[45]

He continues:

In a socialist Tanzania, then, our agricultural organization would be predominantly that of cooperative living and working for the good of all. This means that most of our farming will be done by groups of people who live as a community and work as a community. They would live together in a village; they would farm together; and undertake the provision of local services and small local requirements as a community. Their community would be the traditional family group, or any other group of people living according to Ujamaa principles, large enough to take account of modern methods and the twentieth-century needs of man.

The land this community farmed would be called "our land" by all the members; the crops they produced on that land would be "our crops"; it would be "our shop" which provided individual members with the day-to-day necessities from outside; "our workshop" which made the bricks from which the houses and other buildings were constructed, and so on . . .

For the essential element in them (Ujamaa communities) would be the quality of all members of the community, and the members' self-government in all matters which concerned only their own affairs. For a really socialist village would elect its own officials and they would remain equal members with the others, subject always to the wishes of the people.[46]

Nyerere was not oblivious to the fact that the society he had in mind could not be established by sheer force. "Viable socialist communities can only be established with willing members," he says. He recognized, though, the importance of action and example; moral persuasion was not enough:

It would also be unwise to expect that established farmers will be convinced by words—however persuasive. The farmers will have to see for themselves the advantage of working together and living together before they trust their entire future to this organization of life. In particular, before giving up their individual plots of land, they will wish to see that the system of working together really benefits everyone.[47]

Lastly, "how to share out as well as how much to grow, the arrangements for the children, the crippled and old—must be made by the agreement of all the participants. Village democracy must be open from the beginning: there is no alternative if this system is to succeed."[48]

The fact that Ujamaa itself ultimately failed should not detract from Nyerere's argument. His thoughts run deep, transcending the drudgery of marxist state socialism. (See Chapter five for an explanation of Ujamaa's failure.)

*   *   *

As for outright anarchist movements, there have existed and still exist anarchist groups in South Africa—notably the Anarchist Revolutionary Movement in Johannesburg, and the Durban-based Angry Brigade. South Africa's pioneer anarcho-syndicalist organization, however—known as the Industrial Workers of Africa—lasted only from 1915 to 1922. It was modeled along the lines of the IWW (Industrial Workers of the World), and it operated mainly among black workers.[49] It is in South Africa that anarchist currents remain strongest in Africa.

There is also organized anarchist activity in Nigeria. The Axe, in the 1980s, though basically stillborn, was a leftist coalition with anarchist tendencies. It predated The Awareness League, which has existed since 1990 as a social libertarian and anarchist movement. Anarchist currents also exist in parts of Zimbabwe, Egypt, Ghana, and elsewhere.

1. Rubin, L. and Winstein, B. *Introduction to African Politics: A Continental Approach.* New York: Praeger, 1974. Pp. 5-7.
See also Horton, R. in Ade Ajayi, J.E. and Crowder, M. (eds.) *History of West Africa,* Volume 1, Second Edition, Longman, 1976, p. 75.
2. See Horton n Ade Ajayi and Michael Crowder, pp. 72-78.
3. Rodney, W. *How Europe Underdeveloped Africa.* Enugu, Nigeria: Ikenga Publishers, 1984, p. 49.
4. Ibid., p. 51.
5. Molema, S.M. in *Readings in African Political Thought,* Gideon-Cyrus, Mutiso, M. and Rohio, S.W. (eds.) London: Heinemann, 1975, p. 45.
6. Azikiwe, N. *Ideology for Nigeria.* Lagos: Macmillan, 1980, p. 7.
7. Ajayi and Crowder, Op. Cit., p. 101.
8. Ibid., pp. 100-101.
9. Ibid., p. 102.
10. Ibid., pp. 94-95. See also Walter Rodney, p. 45.
11. Ajayi and Crowder, Op. Cit., pp. 96-97.
12. Ibid., p. 97.
13. Op. Cit., p. 48.

14. Bohannan, P. *Social Anthropology*. New York: Holt, Rinehart & Winston, 1963, p. 282.
15. Op. Cit., p. 56.
16. Isichei, E. *A History of the Igbo People*. Macmillan, 1976, p. 20.
17. Adapted from lecture mimeographs on African political systems.
18. Op. Cit., p. 21.
19. Ibid., p. 21.
20. Adapted from lecture mimeographs.
21. Fortes, M. and Evans-Pritchard, E.E. (eds.) *African Political Systems*. London: Oxford University Press, 1940, pp. 239-271.
22. Williams, G. in Gutkind, P. and Waterman, P. (eds.) *African Social Studies*. London: Heinemann, 1977, p. 286.
23. Onimode, B. *Imperialism and Underdevlopment in Nigeria*. London: Zed Press, 1982, p. 42.
24. Lubeck, P. in Goldfarnk, W. (ed.) *The World System of Capitalism*. Beverly Hills: Sage Publications, 1979, p. 191.
25. Magubane, B. in Gutkind, P. and Wallerstein, I. (eds.) *The Political Economy of Contemporary Africa*. Beverly Hills: Sage Publications, 1976, p. 176.
26. Ake, C. *A Political Economy of Africa*. New York: Longman, 1981, p. 33.
27. Goncharov, L. in Gutkind and Waterman, op. Cit., p. 176.
28. Magubane, Op. Cit. p. 169.
29. Ake, Op.Cit., p. 139.
30. Williams, Op. Cit., p. 291.
31. Ibid., p. 285.
32. Azikiwe, Op.Cit., pp. 63-65.
33. Ibid.
34. Ibid.
35. See Kropotkin, P. *Anarchism and Anarchist Communism*. London: Freedom Press, 1987.
36. Adapted from lecture mimeographs.
37. Fanon, F. *The Wretched of the Earth*. London: MacGibbon and Kee, 1965, pp. 87-117.
38. Adapted from lecture mimeographs.
39. Fanon, Op. Cit., pp. 29-74.
40. Ibid., p. 29. See also Fanon in Gideon-Cyrus, Mutiso, M. and Rohio, S.W. (eds.) *Readings in African Political Thought*, p. 252.
41. See Nyerere, J. *Freedom and Unity*. Oxford University Press, East Africa, 1969, pp. 162-171.
42. Ibid., p. 163. See also Nyerere in Mutiso and Rohio, Op. Cit., p. 513.
43. Mutiso and Rohio, Op. Cit., p. 513.
44. Ibid., p. 515.
45. Ibid., pp. 534-535.
46. Ibid., pp. 539-540.
47. Ibid., p. 541.
48. Ibid., p. 542.
49. This information is from a letter to the authors by Alfred Jack Cooper, Jr., a South African anarchist.

4

The Development of Socialism in Africa

We touched briefly on the atypical development of classes in a few societies in pre-colonial Africa. However, after European contact, class formation accelerated. The European powers that invaded and colonized Africa in the late 19th century were fully industrialized capitalist countries that saw in Africa a captive market as well as a source for raw materials for their industries. This was the fundamental reason for colonialism.

The colonizers produced a capitalist economy with some similarities to the economies of their own countries.[1] In Europe, the owners of capital had expropriated the land and other means of production from peasants and artisans, turning them into wage workers. From their labor, the capitalists extracted a surplus which they accumulated and invested in more land, factories, and labor in order to extract more surplus. In this way they expanded wealth and reproduced capitalist social relations at the same time.[2]

As we saw previously, the pre-colonial African mode of production was anything but a capitalist mode of production. To serve their own interests, the European colonizers superimposed capitalism on Africa. This entailed the transformation of African societies from relatively self-sufficient communal agricultural units into units dependent on the larger economies being created.[3] A new division of labor was being forced on Africans leading to new material relationships in the larger society. In the colonies, the horticultural basis of the African mode of production was progressively undermined as villages were forced to grow cash crops for export or provide cheap labor for European plants and mines. This created new classes—new material relationships—within the colonies. In her study of colonial Guinea, for example, R.E. Galli identifies several colonial classes:

1. A new administrative class of Europeans
2. A European class of large landowners
3. A European class of large merchants (the trading firms)
4. A European managerial class

This group formed the bourgeois class, the owners of capital—that is, the owners of the land and means of production. This class was aided by what Galli calls the petit bourgeoisie[4]:

1. Mid-level managers in the state apparatus, on plantations, and in trading and mining companies
2. Colonial professionals (doctors, lawyers, etc.)
3. Some indigenous small shopkeepers and traders

How were African societies incorporated into the colonial capitalist system? First, the nobility and chiefs were co-opted into acting as administrators for the colonists. Galli sees them as an agrarian class, not a capitalist class, because they did not exploit villagers in a capitalist manner. They exploited them, rather, because of their traditional authority over land and labor.[5] They delivered taxes and labor to the colonialists, squeezing the peasantry as much as they could, but not directly expropriating land. (A corollary of this could be cited in Nigeria with regard to aristocratic rulers—the Emiros of northern Nigeria, and the traditional Obas in the southwest.) The nobility and chiefs were the tools used to execute the colonial powers' indirect rule over their African colonies.

There was also a small group of educated Africans whom the French called *assimiles*, mainly sons of chiefs and other notables sent to European cities for an education.[6] They were absorbed as lower-level officials in government and as professionals, and aided the colonial capitalist class in administering and maintaining the social order. A good example of this type is the character Obi Okonba in Chinua Achebe's novel, *No Longer at Ease*.

As mines and factories opened in some African colonies, a small working class came into being. The great mass of the people were, though, still peasants, now producing for urban markets. Lastly, there was what Galli has classified as the "lumpen proletariat," that group of Africans who had become alienated from the land and had gone to the cities in a vain search for work. Without an education, they became beggars, prostitutes, petty traders, and layabouts.

By the early 20th century, much of Africa had come under colonial domination. Several societies on the continent had metamorphosed from their precolonial state into societies with discernible, antagonistic classes. As in all class societies, the dominant European imperial class, in alliance with its local agents, engaged in brutal, wholesale exploitation of local labor. Local labor was exploited to produce raw materials for European industries and to generate enough surplus to run the colonies. The relationship of the dominant and subordinate classes in the colonies typified what has been termed "the colonial situation." This phrase aptly captures the sociopolitical, economic and psychological state of affairs in a colonized society.

In analyzing the growth and development of African anarchism, we shall focus on the currents that acted as a countervailing force against the entrenched capitalist mode of production, both under colonialism and neo-colonialism.

THE TRADE UNION MOVEMENT AND THE LIBERATION STRUGGLE IN AFRICA

Trade unions in Africa did not begin as pure, ideological revolutionary organizations. Rather, they emerged during the colonial period in direct response to the colonial situation. They represented, in the main, a revolt against an imposed, inferior sociopolitical and economic status.

The emergence of African labor unions was a further manifestation of the incorporation of the capitalist mode of production into African economies. This incorporation, as we saw earlier, led to the balkanization of African societies into nations and classes. As the exploitation of the colonies continued under European colonialism, the colonized peoples came to gradually realize that the situation was an impediment to their own freedom. The emergence of labor unions was a manifestation of basic class consciousness among the workers, as well as a response to colonial rule.

The growth and development of trade unions in Africa during the colonial period reflected varying conditions in different societies. In the ordinary colonies, such as Ghana and Nigeria, the unions were less revolutionary than in European-settled colonies such as Algeria, Kenya and South Africa, where strong racial undercurrents brought the contradictions of the colonial situation into sharp focus. We shall next examine in some detail the trade union movements in Nigeria and in South Africa, as representatives of the trade unions in these two colonial situations.

THE NIGERIAN LABOR UNION MOVEMENT

Nigerian workers made their first attempt to assert their rights in 1897, when workers in the Public Works Department protested for three days in August against arbitrary changes in working hours. In defiance of Governor McCallum's threats of dismissal, the workers refused to withdraw their demands, and in the end they obtained some measure of relief through a compromise solution.

The trend toward labor agitation increased in the early 1900s as a result of the worsening nature of colonial government policies. Since there were more workers than the existing industries could employ, employers instituted oppressive employment contracts in which workers were treated like slaves. As Ananaba points out in his book, *The Trade Union Movement in Nigeria*, these contracts laid great emphasis on the obligation to work, while they laid no emphasis at all on the rights of the worker.[7]

At the same time, there was a growing consciousness of racial barriers to economic advancement, and of the great disparities between European and African earnings, even for the same jobs.[8] In the words of Gutkind and Cohen, "the colonial-racial nexus further erode[d] class awareness by stressing the common identity of all Africans in their subordination to and exploitation by an alien hierarchy."[9]

Moreover, the 1929 global depression further aggravated the condition of workers under colonialism, as colonial governments took the opportunity created by economic desperation to impose direct taxation on workers and to convert permanent jobs to day-labor jobs, among other things.[10] That same year, the famous Aba Women's Riot took place, in which women from the southeastern Nigerian town of Aba and surrounding provinces demonstrated against a new tax on their own property. It is instructive that this particular riot, in which many women were killed, was organized and executed by women.[11]

Radicalization of workers in Nigeria continued in the late 1930s, partly due to a growing spirit of working class consciousness and partly, according to Asoba, as a result of Dr. Nnamdi Azikiwe's new brand of combative journalism, which brought to public attention the various forms of colonial exploitation. Azikiwe inspired Nigerians' confidence in their ability to bring colonial rule to an end through activist political and working class agitation.[12] Other manifestations of radical working class consciousness were the observance of May Day celebrations and the establishment of a Workers' Week.[13]

Another factor in the burgeoning of radical trade unionism in Nigeria was the Railway Workers Union, which was the first radical union to organize strike actions. The union's radicalism can be attributed to the "towering and fearless personality of Michael Imoudu."[14] He led Nigerian workers to great victories, the most outstanding of which was the 1945 general strike; there the "solidarity of the labour rank and file"[15] was first truly seen in the Nigerian labor movement. Subsequent strikes arising from the nature of the colonial system strengthened the labor movement challenge to the economic and political status quo.

In 1949, for instance, the tragic Iva Valley coal miners strike took place at Enugu, Nigeria. It resulted in the massacre of dozens of striking miners by the colonial police force; but during the strike the miners managed to sabotage the coal mining process. Such strikes greatly raised the class consciousness of the workers and seeded thoughts of socialism in their minds, opening their eyes to the nature of not only capitalism, but of the government and its laws as well.[16]

The trade union movement in the colonial period also served as a countervailing influence against foreign investors, who dominated strategic parts of the national economy. In Nigeria these investors included domineering transnational corporations like the Lever Brothers, United African Company, and the United Trading Company, all of which maintained a firm grip on the export and import trade. The unions fought collectively against foreign monopoly capital and agitated for the socialization of important industries in the country, with a view to installing a socialist government where the identity of the working class would not be forgotten.[17]

Although the labor movement in Nigeria contributed quite significantly to ending British colonial rule, post-independence Nigeria reflected the same basic sociopolitical and economic structures that existed under colonial rule. In post-colonial Nigeria, workers have had to contend with essentially the same capitalist system, typified by antagonism between capital and labor. Today, the working people of Nigeria are suffering heavily under the burden of unemployment, factory closures, inadequate housing, transport, health care and educational facilities, social insecurity, and lack of personal freedom.

A prominent feature of the post-independence Nigerian labor movement, that distinguishes it from the pre-independence movement, is the clear absence of a revolutionary perspective. Since independence, the unions have exhibited a tendency to act in league with the ruling elite in the running of the state, while mouthing revolutionary jargon.

In 1987, under the military dictatorship of general Ibrahim Babangida, the Nigerian Labour Congress (NLC) participated in a wide-ranging debate on the political future of Nigeria. The workers published a "Workers' Manifesto" titled, "Towards a Viable and Genuinely Democratic Future: [the] Nigerian Working Class Position," containing 28 points relating to political, economic, social and cultural issues."[18] According to the then-NLC president, the document reflected the political aspirations of the Nigerian working class, namely, that "only a socialist option can ensure a viable and stable political and economic arrangement in Nigeria."[19]

The NLC manifesto spoke of raising the political consciousness of the working class, and it called for full working class involvement in political life. The document's position on the future economy is that the working class should plan and control the production and distribution processes. According to the manifesto:

> From taking control of the economy through so-called investments to over-invoicing, we have seen clearly the collaboration of the multi-nationals and their local agents in ruining our economy, perpetrating fraud and corruption and influencing technocrats and administrators in the performance of government business. What Nigeria requires today under the leadership of the working class is to take our destiny into our own hands through the appropriate political action—socialization of the means of production, distribution and exchange.[20]

Unfortunately, there has always been a sharp divergence between theory and practice in the leadership of the Nigerian working class movement. In reality, the leadership of the trade union movement has always shared a class interest with the ruling elite. This has its origin in the pre-independence era, when the leadership of the working class came to regard the nationalist struggle and the cause of the labor movement as indissolubly linked, and thus allied itself with nationalist political parties. Crowther has gone so far as to regard one of the nationalist parties, the National Council of Nigeria and the Cameroons, as more or less a "confederation of trade unions."[21]

In post-independence Nigeria, the romance between the leadership of the trade unions and political parties has blossomed even more. In Nigeria's ill-fated Third Republic, for instance, there were spirited attempts by the labor movement to form a political party under the aegis of the Nigerian Labour Congress to compete against other political parties. When that failed, the leader of the NLC, Paschal Bafyau, along with his supporters, pitched his tent with the Social Democratic Party and contested the party's presidential primaries, which he lost.

As the struggle against military dictatorship gained momentum in Nigeria, there have been some successes. Labor leaders such as Frank Kokori, General Secretary of the National Union of Petroleum and Natural Gas Workers, and Milton Dabibi, General Secretary of the Petroleum and Natural Gas Senior Staff Association (both unions representing workers in the petroleum industry, the country's mainstay), displayed admirable courage in 1994 when they successfully led their unions in strikes which for two months closed oil facilities across the country. When the military government reacted by deploying soldiers to break the strikes, the workers resorted to sabotage. So effective were the strike actions that the country was virtually paralyzed while they lasted. In Lagos, the bustling commercial capital city of Nigeria, streets and major highways were nearly deserted, public transportation grounded, and offices and work places shut down. As reported in *The Lagos Guardian Newspaper*, the Lagos State Military Administrator, Col. Oyinlola, had to walk to the opening of a seminar, having been unable to find gas for his official car.[22]

One interesting and instructive aspect of these strikes was their decidedly political aim—"to bring an end to military dictatorship." In its 72-hour ultimatum to the federal government, the Lagos branch of the NLC demanded the following: 1) that the federal government should immediately and unconditionally release all political and labor activists detained nationwide; 2) that all closed media outlets be reopened immediately; and 3) that the government should immediately enter into meaningful dialogue with workers and all disaffected groups, minorities and disaffected ethnic nationalities.[23]

As the crisis deepened, the NLC in Lagos concluded that "it will be a great disservice to workers in Lagos State if [the] Labour Congress would fold its arms and allow the workers to continue to suffer . . ."[24] Consequently, it directed all Lagos State "workers in banks and insurance firms, factories, and industries, local government councils, public corporations, federal and state civil service, and so on, to embark on a sit-at-home strike as from July 12, 1994 until otherwise directed by the State Council."[25] The anarcho-syndicalist Awareness League took an active part in the strikes and demonstrations, convinced that the departure of the military government would allow greater opportunity to carry on the struggle for a libertarian society. Never since the civil war of the 1960s had the Nigerian state come so close to disintegrating. But the military junta of General Sani Abacha responded by issuing a barrage of decrees proscribing labor unions, arresting activists and labor leaders en masse, and sacking opposition media outlets.

One thing remains clear: despite courageous attempts by the labor movement to revolutionize Nigeria, its efforts were limited in both scope and content. A primary reason is that, being centralized and hierarchical in structure, the unions function as authoritarian, bureaucratic organizations. Their leaders often see their positions as opportunities to feather their own political and economic nests. The NLC desires to see a more humane Nigerian society, but the ideological inspiration that informs the actions of the congress does not contemplate a completely different kind of society, built by the workers organizing in the workplace and in the community. Usually Nigerian labor leaders do not aspire beyond involvement with the powers that be in the running of the economy and the state. Consequently, the activities of the movement are not based on a clear conception of class reality and class struggle. In their world view of a better and freer society, most labor leaders fail to direct their activities against the double yoke of capital and state. This pattern has been typical in the former "normal" colonies, as contrasted with European-settled colonies such as South Africa.

THE SOUTH AFRICAN LABOR MOVEMENT

South Africa stands out as one of the countries in Africa in which labor has played a decisive role in the struggle for significant sociopolitical change. The struggle of the South African working class dates back to the formative years of South Africa—1910 to 1922—when labor engaged in bloody battles with the capitalist class. Gary Jewell's documentation of the conflicts between employers and workers is most instructive. According to Jewell, in the space of a decade the orgy of violence had resulted in a call by the workers for "a red or syndicalist workers' Republic."[26] Although these early workers' revolts were carried out predominantly by white workers, over time some of the strikes began to be initiated by blacks. In 1920, for example, a strike of the Port Elizabeth municipal black workers, organized by Samuel Masabala of the Cape Provincial Native Congress, resulted in the police shooting deaths of 19 workers.[27] This led to a strike in the Rand in which over 40,000 black miners demanded improved career prospects in jobs reserved for whites.[28]

By 1921, Percy Fisher, Secretary of the South African Mine Workers Union, had initiated the formation of a Miner's Council of Action, which developed into a Red International of Labour Unions, with a revolutionary mission. Jewell identifies the four basic factions that constituted the union as follows: 1) the Communist Party, Bolshevik with DeLeonist elements favoring an industrial union government; 2) Afrikaner Mynwerkersbond, consisting of poor white Afrikaners calling for an Afrikaner Union to destroy the British capitalists and establish a republic; 3) Labour Party moderates, led by Archie Crawford; and 4) the old IWW syndicalist network.[29]

Jewell notes that "the presence of independent IWW syndicalists is demonstrated by the government charge that the strike attempted to set up a 'Red or Syndicalist Workers' Republic.'"[30] Jewell's account of the events leading to the declaration of a Red Workers Republic is informative. According to him, the strike action was carried out by workers in different industries, including the South African Industrial Federation's coal miners, later joined by gold miners, engineers, and power workers.

In the face-off between the workers and the rulers, the Smuts government tried hard to break the workers' solidarity, but with little success. When it became clear that the workers remained un-compromising in their demands, Smuts threw the government's military support behind the mine bosses and declared martial law, urging them to reopen the mines.[31] As discussions continued to break down, the Miners Council of Action "seized the initiative and forced the South African Industrial Federation to proclaim a general strike."[32] The declaration of a Red Workers Republic followed the proclamation of a general strike. The Smuts government responded by sending detachments of the army and air force to attack the striking workers. The building housing the strikers' headquarters in Benoni was strafed on the 14th of March, and at least 153 people died in the attack.[33]

It has been argued that because this strike was conducted primarily by white workers with relatively little support from blacks, there was an absence of class solidarity. However, Jewell quotes James Duke's view that the strike and the declaration of a Red Workers Republic was "a major breakthrough in race relations and class struggle, virtually an Afrikaner civil war with black support for the Afrikaner."[34]

The imposition of apartheid in 1948, however, entrenched in South Africa a class war that largely followed racial lines. With the ascendance of apartheid, class identification and class struggle in South Africa became predicated on the color of a worker's skin. This had started two years previously in 1946 when a strike by 60,000 black workers received no support from the all-white Miners' Union, and was quickly crushed by the mine owners and the Smuts government.[35]

By 1956, the Nationalist government had broken up the South African Trades and Labour Council along racial lines—the South African Confederation of Labour was made up of whites, and the Trade Union Council of South Africa was made up of nonwhites (coloreds and Asians).[36] Although apartheid greatly emasculated the workers' movement and polarized workers along racial lines, massive black strikes continued into the 1970s, often aimed at winning pay increases for workers.

But the real impetus for the burgeoning of radical black labor unions under apartheid was the Labour Relations Act of 1981, which gave the unions a measure of recognition and allowed them to operate legally.[37] In 1975, the Progressive Party had declared South Africa the second most strike-ridden country in Africa (after Morocco).[38] But in 1976, Vorster Botha, then prime minister of South Africa, had boasted to German investors that "South Africa was free of strike[s]."[39] But strikes resulted in the loss of 243,000 working days during the first three months of 1988, and a walkout by two to three million workers on June 6th through 8th of that same year was the biggest in South Africa's history.[40] While wages and working conditions were the major causes of the strikes, an aggravating factor was capital's pressure on the regime to reduce the number of jobs in the public sector, restrict wage increases to three percent, and to privatize the economy as a way to solve the country's economic crisis.[41]

The Congress of South African Trade Unions (COSATU), a syndicalist-oriented organization, was launched on November 30, 1985 during the state of emergency of July 1985–March 1986.[42] The National Union of Mine Workers (NUM) was the largest of COSATU's affiliates.[43] We may well say that the glory days of working class struggle in South Africa were brought back to life with the birth of COSATU. In 1986, the labor movement in South Africa, under the leadership of COSATU and with the support of students and community organizations, observed the 100th May Day with a walkout/strike. At the time, it was the largest such action to ever take place in South Africa; over 1,500,000 million workers took part in the call for the day to be declared a public holiday.[44]

Another display of workers' solidarity occurred on October 1, 1986, the day of mourning for the 177 miners who were victims of the Kincross mining disaster. The work stoppage was organized by the National Union of Mine Workers, and 325,000 miners took part.[45]

As a countervailing force against foreign monopoly capital, the unions supported disinvestment from South Africa. The economic sanctions and disinvestment campaigns spearheaded by the unions, and later adopted by many Western governments, contributed in no small measure to the final capitulation of apartheid.

The struggle of the South African working class that preceded the collapse of apartheid showed that many workers were prepared to lose their jobs in the course of the struggle. T.B. Fulani notes that when a black worker in South Africa went on strike, the worker risked not only losing his job, but also losing his home in the city, and being forced into a Bantustan [an economically depressed "homeland" similar to a U.S. Indian reservation—ed.].[46] In spite of a sharp increase in the cost of living, taxation, growing unemployment, and increased repression of trade unionists, the number of strikes in South Africa continued to rise in the years preceding the collapse of the apartheid regime. Fulani summarizes the range of social, economic and political demands of South African labor unions: since 1979 workers have demanded the right to form trade unions of their choice; they rejected all government-created institutions such as community councils and the president's council; they fought against the introduction of a new income tax for blacks in 1984; they demanded the withdrawal of government troops from black townships. They fought against low wages and the victimization of workers; and they organized a boycott of white-owned shops and factories.[47]

Although the working class movement in South Africa can boast of a long history of struggle, this struggle has not fundamentally changed society. In the fight against the apartheid regime, the South African unions were taken over by middle class politicians of the African National Congress (ANC), who lack clear revolutionary political goals. The outcome of this takeover compromised the ideal of a completely different kind of society. The leadership of the unions became an integral part of the reformist struggle of the ANC for majority rule in South Africa. It's no accident that many leaders of COSATU have received plum jobs in the post-apartheid ANC government of Nelson Mandela.

The ANC government does not represent much that is fundamentally new to the working class in South Africa. This is clear to both the ruling elite and to South African workers. The same old capitalist mode of production, based on the exploitation of labor by capital, continues to exist in South Africa. The working class task still remains the revolutionary transformation of society, that is, the achievement of a truly new society based on liberty and socioeconomic equality.

*　　　*　　　*

Socialism or communism as an ideological model is not entirely new to Africa; it first gained ground in South Africa with the formation of the Communist Party in 1921. The South African Communists, who broke away from the Labour Party in 1915 to form the International Socialist League (ISL), had as one of their objectives the pursuit of proletarian internationalism.[48] An editorial in the fourth issue of *The International*, the weekly paper of the ISL, stated on October 1, 1915 that "an internationalism that does not concede the fullest rights which the native working class is capable of claiming will be a sham . . . If the League deals resolutely in consonance with socialist principles with the native question, it will succeed in shaking South African capitalism to its foundation . . ."[49] Thus the International Socialist League made efforts to identify with the workers and with the plight of the down-trodden black population. It made contact with all existing black organizations, such as the African National Congress, and founded the Industrial Workers of Africa trade union.[50]

In 1921, under the auspices of the Third International, the Marxist-DeLeonist ISL accepted Lenin's 21 demands and formed the Communist Party of South Africa. Its leaders were S.P. Bunting, former Labour Party Chairman W.H. Andrews, and direct-action mine workers Ernie Shaw and Percy Fisher. Though it adopted the organizational form of a Bolshevik party, the South African C.P. remained strongly influenced by IWW (Industrial Workers of the World) revolutionary syndicalist views, and by DeLeonist industrial union concepts.[51]

But through the years the South African Communist Party underwent a marked transformation, both in its relationship to the state and in its conception of the struggle for a better society. It abandoned its initial revolutionary program, and in alliance with other nationalist groups conceived and began to work for a two-step approach to liberation, to wit, a bourgeois democratic revolution, followed by a socialist revolution. The party was more concerned with the issue of state power than class power, and paid scant attention to bringing an end to power and privilege in South African society.

The major liberation movements in South Africa—the African National Congress and the South African Communist Party—both adopted a document known as the Freedom Charter as a framework for a liberated South Africa. The Freedom Charter, however, while it proposed to restrict the operations of monopoly capitalism, did not envisage the abolition of the capitalist system. As Sisa Majola states, the Freedom Charter "envisage[d] the development of small-scale capitalist enterprises as a result of the elimination of the various colour barriers."[52] Accordingly, the Charter envisioned a South Africa where all people "shall have equal rights to trade where they choose, to manufacture and to enter all trades, crafts and professions." Majola further observes that even the demand contained in the Charter, that "restriction of land ownership on a racial basis shall be ended, and all the land redivided among those who work it, to banish famine and hunger," did not necessarily propose the socialization of land ownership and control." From all of this we can conclude that the initial ideals which the South African Communist Party embraced were short lived; they were compromised by its alliance with nationalist groups for the purpose of acquiring political power.

THE "REVOLUTION" IN GUINEA

The so-called revolution in Guinea deserves comment in that the party that led the "revolution"—the Democratic Party of Guinea (DPG)—was a mass party with a revolutionary ideology based on worker and peasant interests.

The organization of workers in Guinea was led by Sekou Toure, a descendant of a famous anti-French colonialism resistance leader in the 19th century. Under Toure's guidance, trade unions merged their protest against French rule with that of various ethnic and regional associations, creating the PDG. In its early years, the PDG maintained strong links with the French syndicalist union, the CGT.

The objective of the PDG's founders was to create a mass party, and they achieved this at least for the duration of the independence struggle. The PDG achieved its mass mobilization by appealing to workers on bread and butter issues—salaries, benefits, etc.—and then to peasants on the basis of needs such as roads and schools, and also on the basis of their resentment toward their chiefs and nobility who had sold them out to the French. They particularly appealed to women and to youth, both groups extremely exploited by the elders and chiefs.

Guinea's chiefs were more or less tax administrators for the French, bleeding their own people dry. They also provided forced labor for mines and plantations. They had become discredited among their people, and the PDG exploited this. By 1956, the party had united the country and swept the elections of that year. This caused the French governor to issue a statement that recognized that the chieftaincy "was gravely compromised . . . and it was no longer admissible that we maintain against wind and storm chiefs who no longer represent anything." Following the election, the PDG set up village committees, some of which made up lists of grievances against their chiefs and exacted reparations from them. This frightened many chiefs, who then fled to the capital, Conakry.

In 1957-58, the PDG stripped the chiefs of power and established popularly elected local governments, from the village up. They also began to tax French companies, broke up trading monopolies, and reformed government. When in 1958 the people of Guinea voted for independence, the French fled en masse, and in revenge took with them whatever they could carry, even the telephones from the walls. Only 20 French administrators out of an estimated 41,000 remained. The stage was then set for peasant and worker interests to influence the government and the development of Guinea. But, as in South Africa, this was short lived. The new "revolutionary" politicians soon prostituted the ideals of the liberation struggle, as is inevitable whenever "revolutionary" politicians occupy positions of power and privilege.

THE AWARENESS LEAGUE:
AN AFRICAN ANARCHIST MOVEMENT

The Awareness League began as an informal study group at the University of Nigeria, Nsukka, in the mid 1980s. The group continued to function essentially as a leftist coalition composed of marxists, trotskyites, human rights activists, and leftists and radicals of various persuasions. Until 1989, the group consisted mostly of student activists, journalists, and university graduates. The different tendencies within the body generated intense debates and self-criticism.

This type of group was not without precedent, though. At Ibadan University, a similar left coalition, The Axe, had existed since about 1983. Its members published for a while a periodic newsletter known also as *The Axe*, and later *The Socialist Register*. This group barely survived the crisis that engulfed the left, notably the authoritarian left, in the second half of the 1980s.

The debates that went on within the Awareness League at the end of the 1980s brought to the fore the need to transcend the body's organizational structure—namely, its informality and its seeming absence of a clear ideological direction. This turmoil coincided with the political convulsions in Eastern Europe and the growing unpopularity of marxist socialism around the world.

The eventual collapse of Communism was foreshadowed in a lengthy analysis in *The Torch* newspaper, a monthly publication of the Revolutionary Socialist League in the U.S.A. The former trotskyites at *The Torch* ran a long and thorough repudiation of marxism-leninism and the state socialist systems it had given rise to. Authored by Ron Taber, and titled "A Look at Leninism," the series attempted to show that Soviet-style state socialism was doomed.

Members of the Awareness League study group followed this critique with close interest. Its brutal perceptiveness left most members of the Awareness League in no doubt about the way forward for the League. In response to the series published in *The Torch*, the League wrote, "we are a body of young, unemployed university graduates, students, and artisans, interested in, and committed to, the teachings and principles of socialism. We hold revolutionary socialism as our manifesto . . . We are particularly impressed by the publication, 'A Look at Leninism,' which we consider an important self-critical effort, which no true marxist or revolutionary can afford to wish away."

Subsequent events led to the transformation of the group into an anarchist organization, though it still retained its old name. By February 1, 1990, the Awareness League formally shed its former image as a leftist coalition. The group's charter, approved in 1991, pronounced the League as a:

> social libertarian organization inspired by and committed to the ideals, principles, objectives, goals, ends and purposes of revolutionary socialism and anarcho-syndicalism, characterized as the antithesis of statism as well as the manifestations and institutions thereof.
>
> With capitalism enmeshed in interminable crisis and its institutions—social, economic, political and cultural—increasingly succumbing to fatigue across the globe, the imperative for sustained struggle against the forces of capitalism has never been greater. It is instructive to note that the crisis of capitalism has been most intensive and pronounced in the underdeveloped third world countries. This is not surprising, to say the least: capitalism's chain was bound to break at its weakest links.
>
> The Awareness League upholds the principles and dictates of internationalism, convinced that national boundaries and territoriality are but artificial creations. The League stands for and is committed to peace and rejects war, militarism, fascism, and racism as well as the acquisition and development of technologies that promote war, militarism, and, in turn, undermine peace and peaceful coexistence among nations.
>
> The League advocates violence only as a form of resistance to the violence and violent methods and tactics of the ruling class, its agencies and collaborators or as a form of liberation struggle. To this end, the Awareness League, as an anarcho-syndicalist and revolutionary socialist front, proclaims all over the world and insists that no form of collaboration can exist between the ruling classes—the exploiter—and their victims, the masses.

The League has since grown into a 1000-member movement with members in all 15 southern Nigerian states, as well as the states of Kaduna, Adamawa and Plateau in the north. In 1996 the League was admitted as the Nigerian section of the International Workers Association (IWA), the anarcho-syndicalist international.

1. R.E. Galli, 1982 "Political Economy Lecture," University of Calabar, p. 2.
2. Ibid., p.2.
3. Ibid.
4. Ibid.
5. Ibid.
6. Ibid.
7. Ananaba, W. *Trade Union Movement in Nigeria.* London: C. Hurst, 1969, p. 11.
8. Coleman, J. Nigeria: *Background to Nationalism.* Berkeley: University of California Press, 1971, p. 258.
9. *African Labor History.* London: Sage Publications, 1978, p. 52.
10. Asoba, S.O. "Trade Unions in Colonial and Post-Colonial Nigeria," in *Topics on Nigerian Economic and Social History.* Ile Ife: UNIFE Press, 1960, p. 198.
11. Pauline, Denise. *Women of Tropical Africa.* Berkeley: University of California Press, 1963.
12. Asoba, Op. Cit., p. 198.
13. Coleman, Op. Cit., p. 12.
14. Asoba, Op. Cit., p. 201.
15. Ibid.
16. Ibid.
17. Cohen, R. *Labour and Politics in Nigeria.* London: Heinemann Education, 1974, p. 12.
18. *The African Communist.* No. 109, Second Quarter, 1987, p. 76.
19. Ibid., p. 76.
20. Ibid., p. 77.
21. Crowther, M. *The Story of Nigeria.* London: Western Printing Services, 1962, p. 223.
22. *Lagos Guardian Newspaper,* July 13, 1994, p. 5.
23. Ibid.
24. Ibid.
25. Ibid.
26. Jewell, G. *The Bloody Ground: Class War in South Africa.* 1977, p. 1.
27. Ibid., p. 7.
28. Ibid.
29. Ibid., p. 9.
30. Ibid.
31. Ibid., p. 10
32. Ibid.
33. Ibid., p. 11
34. Ibid., p. 12
35. Ibid., p. 14
36. Ibid.
37. *The African Communist,* No. 111, 1987, p. 86.

38. Jewell, Op. Cit., p. 15
39. *The African Communist*, No. 115, 1988, p. 31.
40. Ibid.
41. Ibid.
42. *The African Communist*, No. 110, 1987, p. 22.
43. Ibid., p. 26.
44. *The African Communist*, No. 108, 1987, p. 49.
45. Ibid., p. 49.
46. The African Communist, No. 106, 1986, p. 82.
47. Ibid.
48. Jewell, Op. Cit., p. 14.
49. Ibid.
50. Ibid.
51. Ibid.
52. *The African Communist*, No. 117, 1989, pp. 91-92.

5

The Failure of Socialism
in Africa

Economic development has been central to the ideologies of post-colonial African states. In their choice of which ideological model to adopt for economic development, some states have chosen a form of socialism—"African socialism," as some of its proponents have labeled it. However, the term "socialism" as used here does not signify a rigid, doctrinaire approach as in marxism-leninism. Thus Senghor identifies "spiritual values" which he feels were lost to Soviet Communists under Stalin; Kwame Nkrumah saw no contradiction between socialism and Christianity; and Julius Nyerere has associated African socialism with traditional kinship solidarity in his Ujamaa concept. Advocates of African socialism postulate that the marxist theory of material determinism should not be applied in Africa, given Africa's vastly different (than European) economic and social conditions. Rather, they call for a decentralized, democratic African socialism, which they trace back to the history and cultures of the African people.

But the concept of African socialism has been severely criticized. Goldthorpe identifies a strong strand of elitism in "African socialism." According to him, where there is socialism in Africa, it has been planned by an elite. Similarly, Paul Sigmund has pointed out that many post-colonial African states see strong government as the only way to achieve modernization and development, and their leaders coin phrases such as Sekou Toure's "democratic dictatorship" to express their belief that the government or ruling party must lead the people. Nkrumah, who advocated African socialism, asserted that his Convention People's Party formed the nucleus of a new Ghanian society. This required that the party "generalize" itself into society. As Nkrumah said, "the CPP is a powerful force, more powerful indeed than anything that has appeared in the history of Ghana. It is the uniting force that guides and pilots the nation, and it is the nerve centre of the positive aspirations in the struggle for African irredentism. Its supremacy cannot be challenged. The CPP is Ghana, and Ghana is the CPP."[1]

The actual policies and the failures of "African socialist" regimes reveal the emptiness of such grandiose, self-serving rhetoric. The African poet Okot aptly captures the failure and tragedy of post-independence African regimes in his article, "Indigenous Ills":

> . . . the most striking and frightening characteristics of all Africa governments is this, that without an exception, all of them are dictatorships, and practice ruthless discrimination as makes the South African apartheid look tame. African Socialism may be defined as the government of the people by the educated for the educated . . . [It is] discrimination by the educated men in power against their fellow men—their brothers and sisters, mothers and fathers, against their own folk left in the villages.[2]

Let us look at some specific instances where African socialism failed to improve the lives of the ordinary people. What happened to the Guinean revolution after independence? Some analysts describe what happened in post-independence Guinea as simply an overreaction; but for a more detailed analysis we turn to Samir Amin's book, *Neo-Colonialism in West Africa*. According to Amin, the first important point is that after independence, the PDG opened itself to the opposition parties that had represented the chiefs. The second important point is that, despite an original democratic organization from the village upward, soon major decisions for the country were made by the general secretary and the executive organ of the political bureau. Thus decision making soon became very centralized. The PDG incorporated all organizations, including trade unions and women's organizations, into its fold, thus concentrating power at the top.

Given all this, it's obvious that the Guinean peasantry had little impact on government decisions. As we have seen, decisions were executed by a cadre of the few African civil servants educated by the French, and by a number of expatriates. In the first three-year plan, the peasants were to be organized into cooperatives, and the government was to establish a number of state farms using modern techniques; but by 1970, Amin could report no serious start on cooperative organization, and the plans for cooperatives were

subsequently dropped. He also reported that agricultural modernization had not proceeded at all.

R.E. Galli cites two factors for the failure of the Guinean revolution.
One was the over-centralization of the party in the post-independence
period. Second, and more fundamentally, the government and party
deliberately chose to rely on mining as opposed to agriculture as the
economic base of the country. From the moment that it achieved
power, the PDG moved to ally itself with mining companies in the
hands of foreign capital. According to Galli, the party saw the mines
as its opportunity to extract an economic surplus with which to
maintain the state and to keep the PDG in power, because the mines
could provide an income source independent of peasants and
workers, and the PDG could thus afford to ignore their interests.

However, despite its ventures into mining, Guinea today remains
one of the poorest countries in the world. The United Nations has
designated it as one of the 31 least-developed countries; and it has a
very low GNP. Guinean workers, as one might suspect, have not fared
well—throughout the 1970s and 1980s real wages fell as inflation rose.

The purpose of examining Guinea here is not to paint a complete
picture of its political economy, but to lay bare the sham of African
socialism and, in particular, the role of the state in it. The lessons to
be learned from Guinea are:
1) There can be no development of Africa that does not raise the
productivity and income of peasants, skilled and nonskilled workers,
who form about 90% of the economically productive population of
sub-Saharan Africa. Any development policy that aims at meaningful
change must touch the lives of the poor majority.
2) The reliance on state power over workers and peasants directly
contributes to Africa's underdevelopment.
3) A successful agricultural production process will be based on the
workers and peasants themselves running things (voluntary collectivi-
zation), the elimination of the profit motive, and the appropriate
application of technology.[3]

Tanzania provides another pertinent case study of a country whose
leaders dedicated themselves to rural development shortly after
achieving independence (from Britain). Julius Nyerere, head of the
Tanzanian government, was one of the foremost exponents of African
socialism and the principle of self-reliance. In 1979 he addressed the
World Conference on Agrarian Reform and Rural Development,
stating that:

Rural development means development. It indicates an approach and the order of priorities. It involves every aspect of government and social activities. It means acting to reverse the traditional flow of wealth from the rural areas into the towns and forcing that wealth into channels which will benefit the workers who actually produce it with their hands and brains. It means transferring to the poorer and rural areas some of the wealth produced in the richest economic sectors. In practically all developing countries these things require a revolution in the present patterns of government expenditure and taxation. They will be done if, and only if, the people can organize their own power in their own interest.

Has Tanzania practiced what Nyerere preached? To answer this question, let's look at the story of socialism in Tanzania.

Tanganyika won its independence from the British in 1961 after years of struggle led by the Tanganyika African National Union (TANU). TANU was led by teachers, junior civil servants, merchants, rich farmers, white collar workers, salaried employees, shopkeepers —basically the educated and professional classes in the urban areas and rich farmers and merchants in the rural areas. TANU successfully mobilized the peasantry, to which it gave some economic and organizational support. Like the PDG, TANU aspired to be a mass party. In 1964, it organized itself in cell-like fashion in towns and in the countryside. Ten families formed a party cell at the base of the party structure. Organization extended from village to ward to district to region and, finally, to the national level.

The British did not abandon Tanganyika (later Tanzania, after its merger with Zanzibar) as the French did in Guinea, but very few Europeans ever lived in the country. The British owners of capital were indirectly represented by the colonial state and the managers of their plantations and companies. They employed as an intermediary group the Asian commercial class, which included merchants that dealt in importing and exporting, professionals such as lawyers, high state functionaries, and business managers. This Asian intermediary group was comparable to the French middlemen in Guinea. Even after independence the Asians stayed behind in their customary roles.

The rest of post-colonial Tanzanian society may be broken down as follows. There was an Asian class of artisans, white collar workers, small merchants, and even salaried employees. They were higher in rank than their African counterparts. Another class consisted of rich farmers. And still another consisted of mine, plantation, construction, and service workers. This last was a small but important group, though it never exerted any real influence in TANU. The final and most numerous class consisted of peasants, differentiated into middle and poor peasants.

One of the first actions of the new TANU Tanzanian government was to consolidate its power and position against the Asian commercial class. It did this by limiting the latter's scope of activity and by expanding the state sector to take over commercial and industrial enterprises; the state was moving to take over the Asians' intermediary role between the people and the foreign capitalists.

The government also moved against rich farmers who had benefitted most from the cooperatives set up to facilitate marketing. When inefficiencies and corruption became apparent, the government also moved against the cooperatives. And, to consolidate its control, TANU moved against the National Unions of Workers in 1964 after a series of disputes, placing the organization under the control of the Ministry of Labour. After the mid-1960s, Tanzanian workers effectively lost their right to strike.

By the end of the 1960s we can see that the leaders of TANU had limited the economic capabilities and influence of most rivals or potential rivals: the Asian commercial class; the rich farmers; and the working class. The next step was to consolidate their hegemony over these groups and any factions that were not yet under their control.

TANU leaders outlined their relationship with foreign capital and the peasantry in the Arusha Declaration of 1967. The state nationalized land, and it also took control of majority ownership in the major means of production—the banks and the large industrial firms. Did this mean that the Tanzanian state was driving out foreign capital? Did it mean that the state refused to play an intermediary role? No, according to notable scholars such as Colin Leys, John Saul and Michaela Von Freyhold. After all, the state was merely nationalizing the banks and industries, in some cases offering to merge its capital with that of large foreign firms, in effect becoming their partners. According to Von Freyhold, "no national bourgeoisie can any longer afford to ignore the facilities offered by international capital." And, we might note, capital from the World Bank, the United States, Canada, Sweden, Germany, Denmark, even China, as well as Great Britain, poured in to assist in the building of infrastructure, the training of managers, and to foster agricultural and rural development. As of the late 1970s, foreign aid was paying 50% of the government's development budget.

This alliance of national interests with foreign capital did not solve the problem of the government's growing need for an economic base—that is, revenue to support the state and a surplus to invest in development. Nor did it build a political base in the form of a loyal, supportive constituency.

It was against this background that Julius Nyerere turned to the peasantry, which constituted 90% of the population, by preaching a return to the tenets of African communalism. Henceforth, agriculture and the people themselves would become the new bases for development. The government encouraged Tanzanian peasants to form themselves into villages based on cooperation and communal work—the Ujamaa villages. To support this, it would provide social services such as roads, schools, etc. In September 1967, Nyerere published his pamphlet, *Socialism and Rural Development,* in which he spelled out three fundamental traditional principles upheld by the African family: equality, mutual respect for all families, and participation in the benefits of collective production. These were to be the basis of the Ujamaa villages.

Today, there are no surviving Ujamaa villages in Tanzania, only memories of them. The economy is in serious financial and production crisis. Agricultural production continues to decline, and food shortages abound.

In the early 1970s, Gavin Williams wrote a short but very interesting article called "Taking the Part of the Peasants," in which he compared Tanzanian and Nigerian government policies. He found that in both cases the governments considered the peasants the *problem* rather than the solution to raising agricultural productivity. Despite the fact that the one government called itself socialist while the other was avowedly capitalist, both governments focused on outside, particularly foreign, expertise and technology to develop agriculture, and ignored the peasants themselves.

The Ujamaa model failed because it degenerated into state control over the peasants. Through its bureaucrats and technical assistants, the state started to dictate to the peasants what to do and what not to do, what to produce and what not to produce. Soon, too, the World Bank and other aid donors hijacked the program. The government/World Bank/foreign aid strategy was to establish national production targets for each food crop, including export crops such as cotton, coffee, cashew nuts, tea, sisal, and tobacco. The next step was to set regional targets for the crops grown best in each region—a type of regional division of labor. The third step was to communicate these goals to villages through the state apparatus. Whatever the peasants produced was sold to the authorities, and the government controlled the prices. In this way, the state squeezed the peasants for as much surplus as possible. It would have been simply unthinkable to imagine that Ujamaa, in its original, undiluted form, would have succeeded as part of a state system. To that extent, its failure was logical and inevitable.

African socialism has been a failure in other parts of Africa as well. In Ethiopia under Menghistu, for instance, the so-called Workers Party by the late 1980s had failed miserably in its attempt to lay the groundwork for the socialist transformation of agriculture, the attainment of self-sufficiency in food production, and improvement in the standard of living. Although apologists for the regime normally blame these failures on "strong economic links with the capitalist countries . . . [which meant Ethiopia was] hard hit by the worsening economic crisis of the capitalist world,"[4] the crisis stemmed largely from Ethiopia's state capitalism and bureaucratic centralism. It's also worth noting that the Soviet-style Menghistu regime was one of the worst, most murderous human rights abusers ever seen in Africa.

In Mozambique, the ten-year development plan adopted in 1980 by the ruling FRELIMO party proved unsuccessful. This failure was blamed on "foreign aggression through bandit gangs." Nothing was said of the excessive centralism of Mozambique's planning and management, as well as retention of colonial structures inherited from the Portuguese.

In West Africa, the Burkina Faso "revolution" of 1984 came to an end in 1987 with the assassination of Thomas Sankara, its initiator. Although Sankara recognized that the majority peasant population was a key force, he unfortunately had an overtly critical attitude toward the trade union movement and left-wing parties.[5] Sankara's efforts centered on the Committees for the Defence of the Revolution (CDRs). CDRs were organized at all work places and in all neighborhoods and military units, as "defenders" of the revolution; that is—as in Cuba—they functioned as spies for the government and as enforcers of its policies. The CDRs in Burkina Faso, however, did not have the time to develop the efficiency of their Cuban counterparts, which can be considered the backbone (or at least the far-reaching tentacles) of the Cuban repressive apparatus. In his review of the book, *Thomas Sankara Speaks*, Ahmed Azad notes that "no real attempt it seems was made . . . to resolve the issue of the role, functions, duties, and responsibilities of the CDRs and those of the trade union movement."[6]

On October 15, 1987, Sankara was assassinated by his friend and comrade, Blaise Compaore. In justifying the coup, Compaore said that the Burkinan revolution had strayed under Sankara; he compared his "rectification process" with glasnost in the Soviet Union. However, according to Jabulani Mkhatshwa, Compaore's idea of glasnost "is the further class differentiation that is taking place among the people, the creation of the petty bourgeoisie and the import of Mercedes Benz."[7] Jabulani blames Compaore for the implementation of economic policies contrary to the original ideals of the revolution. As we have seen, however, the process of betrayal was already well under way under Sankara.

We can see that the so-called socialist parties and regimes in Africa—both those that led their countries to independence, and those that achieved power in the post-independence period—have not succeeded in changing the lives and fortunes of poor workers and peasants. These regimes have not achieved anything beyond what openly capitalist states have achieved. If anything, they have maintained and expanded the old system of class privilege. The result has been that class antagonisms, instability, and economic crisis confront the continent. As the crisis rages on and the prospect of the radicalization of the masses heightens, African regimes have been compelled to react. Some have turned into full-blown dictatorships and become openly repressive; other have tried one form of structural adjustment or another; and still others have experimented with various forms of electoralism. Yet all these are palliatives aimed at temporarily quelling restive workers and peasants, for whom daily life has become synonymous with misery.

STATE CAPITALISM AND INSTABILITY

It's now time to look at how the fundamentally capitalist state system in Africa has created unstable sociopolitical and economic structures, as well as the prospect of its own collapse. In analyzing the connection between state capitalism and instability in Africa, our primary objective is to demonstrate how the economic manifestations of state capitalism—underdevelopment, dependence, and subordination to foreign interests, plus their concomitants, poverty, illiteracy, and disease—have led to political instability.

The root of African underdevelopment is, of course, the establishment of colonial capitalism. Put differently, Africa's recent economic history is the result of its colonial past, the most significant aspect of which was the displacement of the precolonial African mode of production through the expansion of mercantilist capitalism from

Europe to Africa. As we have seen, during the struggles for national liberation, the fundamental economic relationships established during the colonial period were not generally seen as detrimental to the interests of the developing nations. Nationalism in Africa was thus primarily limited to the elimination of outright foreign political domination, and the granting of political independence witnessed the perpetuation of class antagonisms and the emergence of an indigenous ruling elite.

In accounting for the instability of present-day African political systems, Professor Claude Ake argues that there are strong revolutionary pressures against the existing exploitative class relations, and thus against the very survival of the ruling elite and the state. He attributes these pressures to, first, the desperate poverty of African workers; second, the huge economic and social discrepancy between rich and poor; third, rising expectations due to modernization; fourth, the enticing models provided by the developed countries, made even more piquant by their portrayals in the media and by the limited penetration of consumer goods and retail firms into African markets; and fifth, the politicization of the African peoples through their frustrating colonial and post-colonial experiences.

Ake notes that the African people are essentially demanding two things. The first is equality, which, in effect, means the abolition of post-colonial capitalism and its privileged classes. The second is "social well-being, . . . easing the agony of extreme want."[8] Ake, however, postulates that neither of these demands will be granted by African ruling elites because "the very condition of underdevelopment very drastically limits the expansion of the economic surplus." Thus the capitalists cannot react favorably to revolutionary pressures without committing class suicide, which, of course, they will not do. According to Ake, this leaves them the option of trying to discourage such demands, while preventing their political manifestations. This is what Ake means when he refers to "depoliticization."

According to Ake, the primary manifestation of depoliticization in Africa is the preaching by African regimes of one-party-state ideologies; this, of course, tends to make African regimes particularly repressive. In Ake's view, "every African country is in effect a one-party state in the sense that every regime in Africa assumes its exclusive right to rule and prohibits organized opposition." Moreover, "given the contradictions in contemporary African society, depoliticization cannot be carried out without brutal repression."

In considering the effects of depoliticization on African regimes, it could be argued that, since depoliticization helps maintain existing class structures, it promotes "political stability."[9] Here, "political stability" means the persistence of the political structure, especially the relationship between the dominant and subordinate classes. Depoliticization in this sense enhances the stability of regimes when it leads to the homogenization of the exploiting classes. "Depoliticization increases homogenization by imposing ideological unity, by building alliances between factions, by co-opting dangerous opponents into the hegemonic faction and by liquidating certain other factions altogether."

On the other hand, depoliticization may actually accentuate governmental instability. In fact, Ake postulates that "on balance, the intra-class depoliticization is more conducive to government instability than to stability." He attributes this to the fact that "it greatly reinforces the destabilizing effect which statism produces by focusing the ambition of all the factions of the exploiting class primarily on the capture of state power, by making the outcome of the struggle for hegemony among the factions of the bourgeoisie too important."[10] In effect, suppression in the political arena does not eliminate the crisis in society. Even with the depoliticization of the masses or the establishment of a one-party system, instability remains because the objective basis of the differences between factions in society remain. Thus, pressures mount, with explosive social tensions between groups in the system. "When major differences in this political monolith appear, a crisis invariably occurs."[11] The options for resolving these differences are drastically limited, according to Ake, because they arise from the substructure. The rulers are obliged to use coercion, but this only worsens the unstable political situation, creating opportunities and conditions that facilitate military intervention.

THE MILITARY FACTOR

In the view of Peter Harris, the widening gulf between the progressively impoverished majority and the privileged few generates the potential for crises in African political systems.[12] Describing the present character of African political developments such as the phenomenon of military coups, Harris recalls that Franz Fanon had predicted as far back as the 1950s that the African middle and professional classes who led the national independence movements would increasingly turn their backs on the people and instead align themselves with foreign interests.

In *Class Conflict in Africa*, Markovitz argues that a fundamental reason for the ease of military takeovers across the continent was that the politicians represented only the privileged.[13] He agrees with Ruth First that in the absence of a socially rooted, economically productive base, "power lies in the hands of those who control the means of violence. It lies in the barrel of a gun, fired or silent."

According to Harris, as the corruption and profiteering of the ruling class have become more blatant, and the stagnation of African economies has reached the point of national bankruptcy, popular discontent has become widespread. As a result, many regimes have discarded their populist smokescreens. This, combined with popular discontent, has set the stage for military takeovers. As Fanon had forewarned, when the discontent of the peasantry and the workers grows, and the regime is forced to resort to harsher measures of rule, "it is the army that becomes the arbiter. . . ."[14] According to Harris, military officers corps, an important segment of the local ruling class, enter the center of the political arena by replacing discredited politicians, thereby preventing the mobilization of the people. The military assume power not only to preserve the continued dominance of the local privileged class, but also to protect the neocolonial interests of the former mother country and of multinational corporations. As Fanon puts it, "the ranks of the decked-out profiteers whose grasping hands scrape up the bank notes from a poverty-stricken country will sooner or later be men of straw in the hands of the army cleverly handled by foreign experts. In this way, the former metropolitan country practices indirect government, both by the bourgeoisie that it upholds and also by the national army. . . ."[15]

Harris and Murray have also analyzed how the grave economic problems of post-independence African regimes have caused the decline of populist nationalist parties and of the charismatic national leaders that led the struggle for independence. Harris believes that the nationalist parties and one-party rule have become obsolete forms of protecting the interests of international and local capitalists due to the combination of predatory economic structures and the growing awareness of elite corruption. Murray attributes this to the deplorable economic conditions in Africa, growing political cynicism, and the abiding human quest for freedom in the social, economic, and political spheres. He argues that this decline is a direct result of the effects of economic stagnation, urban inflation, the ossification of the nationalist parties, and the rapacity of the ruling elites.[16]

Murray argues that because of the political and economic situation, many post-colonial governments have been unable to deal with growing contradictions in their societies, and have had difficulty legitimizing their authority. As a result, both foreign and internal pressures have provoked changes from civilian to military rule. According to Murray, the corruption and incompetence of the nationalist politicians have added to the "fringe costs" of economic activity in these states, and are undermining the function of these regimes as "political holding companies" for foreign capital. The military, on the other hand, has offered "a more effective alternative to foreign capital and to the local bourgeoisie not directly benefitting from the discredited regimes."[17]

So, typically, the military intervenes and comes to power on the crest of rising public discontent, particularly over economic downturns, and the corruption and decadence of the political leadership. They succeed in turning the moral outrage of the people to their own advantage and justify their seizure of power by pointing to the corruption and inefficiency of the politicians. Kenneth Grundy states that, under the initial euphoric state of affairs that attends most military interventions, the military succeed in raising the expectations of the masses over and above their ability to deliver.[18] This strategy, of course, produces a time bomb.

In the long run, military regimes appear even less capable of winning popular support than the civilian regimes that they replace. Because of the time bomb of impossible-to-meet rising expectations, the military are ultimately forced either to resort to repressive measures and risk a counter coup or to relinquish power to a new set of civilians. Because of the reluctance of military regimes to give up power, this often sets in motion a vicious cycle of coups and counter coups, and helps "to bring into clearer focus the social and political crisis of neo-colonial society."[19] According to Harris, this crisis stems from the fact that "the small local bourgeoisie (including its military component) have neither the economic power nor the support of other social strata to stabilize their position of domination and privilege." Consequently, they are forced to rely on repressive measures. This "advances both the critical consciousness of the subordinate classes and the polarization of African society."

POLITICAL CORRUPTION AND SOCIAL INSTABILITY: CASE STUDIES OF GHANA AND NIGERIA

Because of its role in creating instability in African states, political (official) corruption is directly associated with, and almost synonymous with, the state system. The existence of the state and the manipulation of the structures and institutions of the state by the ruling elite for the (mis)allocation and (mal)distribution of public goods and services inevitably leads to corrupt practices. Levine defines political corruption as the "unsanctioned, unscheduled use of public political resources and/or goods for private, that is, non-public, ends."[20] In Africa, the coup d'etat is often preceded by the instability generated by political corruption.

In Ghana, the populist Convention Peoples Party (CPP) government of Kwame Nkrumah was more or less a conglomeration of divergent interest groups, some of which were more concerned than others with the plunder and expropriation of national wealth. To this end, it is pertinent, as Professor Card points out, to distinguish between the CPP leadership and the CPP membership in order to discern what Card terms the "class" basis of the party.[21] The tendency to see the CPP throughout its 15 years as an undivided entity has blurred this distinction.

As Card points out, many members of the CPP leadership began their careers as independent radicals "with little or nothing to lose, in the Fanonist sense." However, over the years, many of the early CPP leaders gained access to wealth and power via the state, "and differences in purely personal interests began to be reflected in differences over policy matters related to the extent and pace of Ghanaian socialism." By 1960, when inner party purges of the old leadership began in earnest, some of the formerly "radical" leaders had become wealthy men, whose prosperity was "linked to the state and foreign capital."

The political corruption of the CPP began in the 1950s, when the party began to consolidate its hold over the population and over the centers of economic and political power. It organized party branches throughout the country, set up a variety of auxiliary organizations, and began to move its people into key positions in various government agencies. Levine cites as an example what happened when the party managed to gain control of the Cocoa Purchasing Company (CPC), formed in 1952 as an agency of the Cocoa Marketing Board. A 1956 investigation of the CPC revealed that the CPP had used the CPC's control of agricultural loans, bulk purchasing, and transportation to enrich party coffers, to coerce farmers into joining the party, and to control petty commerce that was dependent on cocoa. By 1961, accusations of corruption among the party leadership had grown too loud to ignore, but even Nkrumah's much-celebrated "Dawn Broadcast" of April 8, 1961—in which he denounced official corruption and self-seeking—did not break the cult of corruption that had gripped the party and the state bureaucracies. Ocran charges that corruption had become institutionalized in high places and among Nkrumah's minsters and followers in the CPP.[22] He mentions a report of the commission of inquiry into the affairs of the National Development Company which found that it was "established ostensibly to finance the CPP, but that it later became a clearing house for bribes paid to the party or to Nkrumah personally." Ocran concludes that "Ghanaians both inside or outside the party were having a field day chopping Ghana small, without any let or hindrance whatsoever."

The above occurred under the "socialist" government of Kwame Nkrumah, at the time considered the beacon of hope for the decolonizing countries in Africa. In Nigeria, shortly after independence on October 1, 1960, the young state came perilously close, first to collapse, then to constitutional chaos and a bloody civil war. The upshot was a rapid succession of civilian and military regimes. In the late 1970s under General Olusegun Obasanjo, a constituent assembly was set up to write a constitution for the country. In 1979 it produced a constitution which ushered in the civilian government of Alhaji Shehu Shagari.

Like previous Nigerian civilian and military governments, Shehu Shagari's regime was a showpiece of corruption. Ill-conceived bills slid their way through the national legislature lubricated by bribes. Under Obasanjo and then Shagari, the Nigerian government lost millions of dollars to fraud; an example under Shagari was a $20 million (Nigerian dollars) fraud loss by the Federal Housing Corporation.[23] Another instance was the sale of 4,000 bags of rice to ruling party bigwigs at $6.00 per bag. They then resold the rice for between $60 and $90 per bag. An aggrieved permanent secretary in the upper chamber of parliament mentioned senior public functionaries—past and present—as some of the beneficiaries. He alleged that import licenses were given to 121 persons for 255,350 tons of rice, and that President Shagari took 200,000 tons for himself.[24]

A year after the multi-storey Republic Building in Lagos went up in flames, the Audit Division of the Federal Capital Territory was similarly razed. The incident was connected with a $15 million (Nigerian) fraud involving department payment vouchers. Another example of fraud was that reported in late 1982, in which five top officials of the Nigerian External Telecommunications Company were arrested for a $53 million fraud. These incidents are only the tip of the iceberg in the corruption that engulfed the Shagari regime shortly before the military coup on December 31, 1983.

Corruption and theft of public funds by public officials have since become a way of life in Nigeria, as every regime struggles to "better" the record of its predecessor in office. This reached its apex under dictator General Ibrahim Babangida who, along with his aides, salted away billions in overseas bank accounts. General Abacha, the man who succeeded him, is no less corrupt.

Is there any causal relationship between the two variables—political corruption and socioeconomic instability—in African states? Joseph Nye, in his article, "Corruption and Political Development: A Cost-Benefit Analysis," argues that, so far as corruption destroys the legitimacy of political structures, it contributes to instability and quite probably leads to national disintegration. In many African states, "corruption contribute[d] to the aura of disillusion that preceded coups and made it impossible for the regimes to find popular (or elite) support when the chips [were] down."[25]

Nye notes that "one of the most important functions of government is to provide goods and services to qualified recipients on a regular, predictable basis."[26] According to him, there are two problems in the allocation of goods and services through politically corrupt relationships. First, they tend to be selectively allocated, not on the basis of need or utility, but on the basis of personal ties; second, that such allocation tends to be "unreliable because the goods themselves are closely tied to the political fortunes and positions of the distributor [or] office holder." Individuals or groups who do not find themselves in any of the distributive networks get left out altogether, or, at best, are marginalized.

Against this background, one can see that in corrupt capitalist/ statist political systems, the distribution of political goods and services both creates social inequalities and exacerbates those that already exist. In Africa, the gap between the haves and the have-nots has continued to widen since independence, with the lot of both majority and minority ethnic groups deteriorating. It's little wonder that both groups have become alienated and cynical. For example, Nkrumah's "Dawn Broadcast" was privately derided by his colleagues and critics, and was received with cynicism by the public, because the corruption of the regime was by then too patent to be concealed.

The net impact of all this is a rejection of government and the political process by Africa's poor majority, and the intensification of revolutionary pressures around the continent.

STRUCTURAL ADJUSTMENT, ELECTORALISM AND AFRICA'S FUTURE

The introduction of the International Monetary Fund's (IMF's) Structural Adjustment Program (SAP) in the mid-1980s was a clear signal, if any were needed, that post-independence African regimes have not severed the bonds of imperialism. Despite the fact of political independence, African states are still closely tied to international capitalism.

Foreign control of African economic policies is facilitated by the massive indebtedness of African regimes to American and European governments and financial institutions. As Ablaye Diagne, a lecturer in economics at the University of Senegal, has stated, "the debt is one of the mechanisms through which the African countries have again fallen under the yoke of the most ferocious imperialist exploitation."[27]

Diagne identifies some of the causes of this massive indebtedness as: 1) the way in which African countries are integrated into the international capitalist division of labor; 2) the economic policies followed within that framework; 3) in particular, the forms of indebtedness and the use of resources borrowed from abroad; 4) the armaments race, into which Africa has been plunged by imperialism; and 5) debt rescheduling policies.

Because of the economic crises facing them, many African governments have had no choice but to borrow from financial institutions such as the World Bank and IMF. A standard IMF package often involves, among other things, the following "conditionalities": 1) devaluation of currency; 2) tight monetary and fiscal constraints; 3) budget cuts, with sharply reduced public expenditures; 4) a wage freeze; and 5) sharp reduction or elimination of import and price subsidies.

Chinweizu argues that the IMF medicine administered to cure a country's liquidity headache almost always worsens the illness. This is mainly because the IMF "treatment" is designed to help countries with strong industrial bases—countries that can overcome liquidity problems through more competitive pricing of their industrial goods. But for African countries, with weak or nonexistent industrial manufacturing bases, the IMF solution does nothing but stimulate more raw material exports at low prices into a weak world commodity market.

Nevertheless, African governments have had no alternative to bankruptcy other than to borrow from the World Bank and IMF and to introduce the harsh austerity measures they demand. Ethiopia, for example, introduced austerity measures in 1985 while Menghistu drained the national treasury on military expenditures; and Nigeria first introduced full-blown austerity measures in 1981 under the corrupt Shagari regime, and then again in 1986 through the World Bank/IMF Structural Adjustment Program.

The imposition of austerity measures has had far-reaching consequences in many African countries. Rather than ameliorate economic problems, these "adjustment" policies exacerbate them. Rising unemployment, inflation, a soaring cost of living, and other worsening social conditions give lie to the assumptions of SAP. Its social consequences alone are a strong goad to a revolutionary consciousness among Africa's working class; but with the potential radicalization of this sector of African society comes the prospect of the return of military governments to protect the privilege of both foreign and local elites.

Apart from the prospect of military intervention, some African regimes have introduced constitutional conventions as a means of sabotaging the burgeoning of radical consciousness. Such a convention was employed with telling effect in Benin, where President Mattew Kerekou passed the political baton to Nicephore Soglo. Nigeria is the latest example in Africa where the government set up a constitutional convention to obviate the prospect of radical change.

Constitutional conventions normally prescribe electoralism as the way to alleviate a country's problems. But electoralism in Africa is merely a diversionary tactic used to mask the transfer of power from one group of exploiters to another. The fact that dictators in countries such as Congo, Ethiopia, Angola, Mozambique, and Malawi have lately installed multi-party electoralism is evidence that it leads to nothing really new. As elsewhere, electoralism in Africa does nothing to fundamentally change the status quo; it does nothing to abolish the system of privilege and class differentiation. It seems obvious that at this point electoralism carries no redemptive prospects for Africa. The success rates of the various "democratizing" political movements in Africa on such minimal programs as human rights and the rule of law are nothing to write home about.

The introduction of SAPs and constitutional conventions have coincided with the collapse of marxist-leninist socialism the world over. Africa has witnessed the collapse of communist dictatorships in Ethiopia, Benin, and Somalia; and socialist regimes in Zimbabwe, Mozambique, and Angola are tottering and have sought respite by opening their economies to foreign trade and investment, and by allowing "free market" forces to operate. The point is, however, that the collapse of so-called African socialism does not translate into a triumph of capitalism, because African capitalism itself is enmeshed in deep crisis. Rather, it is a vindication of the anarchist critique of both private/corporate capitalism and of state capitalism masquerading as socialism.

The current crisis in Africa thus affords anarchism an historic opportunity to take firm root on the African continent. In reality, post-colonial Africa has always been in ideological flux, but this flux has increased with the collapse of marxism. The majority of post-colonial African states have traditionally tended towards the capitalist model only because it was foisted on them as a condition for the granting of political independence; due to capitalism's failures, other African states opted for state "socialism," which likewise failed to deliver the goods. This leaves Africa with an alternative model of development that will confront the present crisis of hunger, poverty, and disease by ensuring that Africa's productive capacity no longer remains under the control of capitalist or governmental ruling classes.

Today, the military in Africa make no pretense of offering an alternative to capitalism or to state "socialism." If anything, most military men are well aware that they are very much part of the crisis facing the continent. Gone are the days when Eurocentric scholars painted the African military as an alternative agent of modernization or development. Today, African military regimes know that the magnitude of the crisis facing the continent is beyond the capacity of their much-vaunted organizational capabilities. It is finally becoming widely recognized that military intervention in African states is fundamentally reactionary, a temporary aberration that serves to roll back the gains of the poor in their struggle against ruling elites. The way this works is as follows:

Upon coming to power, the military imposes martial law in an attempt to hold together the disintegrating state structure. As the crisis continues unabated in spite of military repression and dictatorship, the military regime is forced to announce dates for elections and the return of the civilian ruling elite. In reality, this is a vicious circle: elections lead to a corrupt civilian government, followed by military intervention, followed by elections leading to a corrupt civilian government, and so on and so forth.

In sum, both civilian and military regimes in Africa represent a mere transitional phase in the march toward a society which will fulfill the human aspirations for liberty, equality, and a humane standard of living. Throughout Africa, the enormous sociopolitical and economic tragedy that has been the continent's lot since its first contact with capitalism and the state system continues to deepen. It is against this background that we postulate an inevitable new social order which will entail the reorganization of social life on the basis of libertarian communism, the abolition of states and political parties, the disappearance of monopoly control of property, and the elimination of all forms of domination. This will be achieved through the establishment of economic communes and administrative organs run by African workers and peasants themselves in their workplaces, forming a system of free, voluntary councils which will not be subject to authoritarian control by any government or political party.

THE HUMAN RIGHTS QUESTION

The human rights records of African countries—be they military (Nigeria), "socialist" (Zimbabwe, Libya), or bourgeois democratic (Kenya, Ghana)—have never been worse than they are today. This is in spite of the bourgeois democratic current currently sweeping the continent. Usually, the facade of elections is the only significant feature of the transition from an authoritarian, one-party state dictatorship to a multi-party "democracy." Even the most minimal human rights agenda is almost always lost in the shuffle.

In Nigeria, for example, the number of political prisoners detained without trial in the past five years has risen significantly to over 1000 at any given time. Several detainees lose their lives daily in prisons and police dungeons nationwide, sometimes without any record of their arrests, detention, or deaths. The Nigerian government regularly closes or bans newspapers and other publications that it considers critical. Nothing, perhaps, better captures the Hobbesian state of Nigeria than the uncanny ease with which the military authorities promulgate decrees and edicts that override the regular courts, especially the notorious preventive detention Decree No. 2 that removes the jurisdiction of the courts over the indefinite detention of persons.

Those suffering long terms of confinement since 1991 include labor leaders, political activists, students, and politicians. These include four members of the Awareness League detained in 1992 and not released until March 1993. Nigeria's military rulers have since proscribed all labor unions, dissolved their leadership, and frozen their assets. The massive repression in Nigeria is matched only by the climate of insecurity that pervades the country because of the criminal activities of armed robbers, the desperately unemployed, and outright gangsters.

Similarly, in Libya hundreds of political prisoners, including prisoners of conscience, are held in detention centers for reasons and/or under conditions contrary to international human rights standards. A report compiled by Amnesty International (MDE 19/03/92) puts the number of political prisoners in Libya in 1992 at 554, an increase of 127 over the previous year's figure. Some of these prisoners have been held since 1974.

Like Nigeria, Libya has signed relevant international protocols on human rights, including the African Charter on Human and People's Rights. These prohibit torture and other cruel, inhuman, or degrading treatment. Unfortunately these accords have done little or nothing to curtail human rights abuses by this "Arab socialist" state. Zimbabwe is another "socialist" state with a poor record on human rights. Under Robert Mugabe's 17-year rule, state-sponsored harassment and intimidation of political opponents and the stifling of labor unions has been routine. And in Algeria the populace is held hostage in a virtual state of terror between an authoritarian military government and a murderous Islamic fundamentalist opposition.

The situation in the newly emerging "democracies" in Africa, namely Kenya, Ghana and the Ivory Coast, is not markedly different. Human rights violations in these places are systemic, thus enabling the authorities to invoke constitutional and legal provisions. Ghana under Jerry Rawlings has literally decimated the opposition. In Kenya, Arap Moi is engaged in an ethnic cleansing campaign against some nationalities, notably the Kikuyu and the Luo. And in nominally democratic Egypt, the police are conducting a "dirty war" against a violent, fanatical Islamic opposition.

What emerges is the omnipresence of authoritarian state control—in the new democracies, in the remaining state-socialist outposts, and, of course, in the military-ruled countries. It's extremely unlikely that this situation will change significantly while private/corporate capitalist regimes (civilian or military) and state-capitalist ("socialist") regimes remain in power. The abolition of these regimes and social re-organization based on the anarchistic elements in traditional African societies is the only answer.

1. Goldthorpe, J.E. "The Sociology of the Third World" in *The African Communist* No. 106, Third Quarter, 1986, p. 59.
2. "Indigenous Ills in Socialism in Tanzania," Ibid.
3. Galli, R.E. Lecture on political economy, University of Calabar, 1982.
4. *The African Communist*, No. 117, Second Quarter, 1989, pp. 70-71.
5. Ibid., pp. 82-83.
6. Ibid., p. 83.
7. Ibid., p. 72.
8. Ake, Claude. *Revolutionary Pressures in Africa.* London: Zed Press, 1978.
9. Ibid. p. 79.
10. Ibid., p. 80.
11. Ibid.
12. Harris, R., ed. *The Political Economy of Africa.* New York: Schwenkan Publishing Company, 1975, p. 30.
13. Markovitz, L. *Power and Class in Africa.* New Jersey: Prentice Hall, 1977, p. 306.
14. Fanon, F. *The Wretched of the Earth.* Middlesex, England: Penguin, 1961, p. 174.
15. Ibid.
16. Murray, R. "The Social Roots and Political Nature of Military Regimes," in Gutkind, P.W., ed., *African Social Studies.* London: Heinemann, p. 384.
17. Ibid., p. 385.
18. Grundy, K.W. "The Negative Image of Africa's Military," *Review of Politics*, Vol. 30, 1968.
19. Ibid.
20. Levine, V.T. *Political Corruption: The Ghana Case.* Palo Alto, California: Stanford University Press, 1975, p. 65.
21. Card, E. "The Political Economy of Ghana," in Harris, R., ed., *The Political Economy of Africa.* New York: Praeger, 1969, p. 182.
22. Ocran, A. *Politics of the Sword.* London: Rex Collings, 1977, p. 45.

23. Nigerian Department of Information, Printing Division, Lagos (Audit Report, 1982).

24. *Sunday Concord Newspaper*, October 9, 1983, p. 1.

25. Nye, J. "Corruption and Political Development," in Levine, Op. Cit., p. 65.

26. Ibid.

27. Cited in Levine, Op. Cit., p. 65.

6

Obstacles to the Development of Anarchism in Africa

Anarchist theory, to put it mildly, is seen in Africa as a fringe, leftist ideology; one indication of this is that anarchism usually receives no more than a passing nod in the syllabi of African university classes. This is paradoxical because in no other continent have anarchist tendencies been as strong as in Africa, and because in modern times the prospect of turning mass action into class struggle remains brightest in Africa. We shall now consider some of the factors that have worked against the development of anarchism in Africa.

COLONIAL EDUCATION

One of the unpleasant realities we encountered while writing this book was how little the contemporary African, including the African political or social scientist (who has probably taken a course or two on comparative political ideologies), knows about anarchism. In terms of literature, virtually nothing is to be found on the bookshelves of universities and bookstores. This is not surprising, however; in his critique of marxism, Ron Taber points out that for over 70 years, anarchism was eclipsed by marxism. Nowhere has this subordination of anarchism to marxist "socialism" been more profound than in Africa.

Much of the dearth of anarchist literature in Africa is a result of the colonial educational system and the concomitant hegemony of Western imperialist literature in Africa. Colonial education in Africa did not seek to educate large numbers of students; rather, European educators selected what they considered the cream of the crop for advanced schooling. One result of this is that only a relatively small proportion of Africa's population has been and is literate. A corollary of this was the emergence of an academic elite who considered themselves superior to the rest of the people. Because its philosophical and ideological assumptions were taken from European class societies, and not from communal and relatively unstratified African societies, colonial education was disintegrative rather than unifying.

Traditional African education, in contrast, emphasized the interdependence of individuals within the community rather than competition between them. It instilled a group social consciousness and fostered an egalitarian spirit; this in turn naturally led to an emphasis on common endeavors and the sharing of the products they generated. On the other hand, colonial education emphasized individualism and made social existence competitive. The communal spirit was supplanted by the concept of the isolated self and greed, materialism, and an unbridled desire for domination. Consequently, Africa has become a continent of atomistic, antagonistic, and competitive groups strongly committed to tribal loyalties and dominated by ethnocentric views.

In sum, colonial education has led to a high level of illiteracy in Africa combined with very low political consciousness, even among the educated. Neither Eurocentric nor Afrocentric scholars have researched anarchism as it relates to Africa. This has ensured that anarchism as a systematic body of thought remains an esoteric, if not unknown, subject to many Africans.

THE LEGAL SYSTEM

African legal systems are a hangover from the colonial past. For example, as in other former British colonies, the legal system in Nigeria is simply an imitation of British common law and equity. It views native laws and customs as barbarous to the extent that they do not reflect European standards and value systems.

Colonial laws were formulated essentially to maintain "law and order," and this remains the cardinal aim of post-colonial African laws. This contrasts sharply with the pre-colonial African system of rights and freedoms. Traditional African societies had an intense sense of humanity and respect for human dignity. Pre-colonial Africans enjoyed most of the rights that today would fall under the rubric of civil and political rights, such as freedom of association, freedom of movement, and freedom of expression. Basic economic and social rights, like the right to the use of a piece of land, the right to work, and the right to an education, were also common in traditional African societies. And these rights were recognized and protected. "Adjudication," if it can be called such, typically consisted of a fair "hearing" for opposing parties before the entire village or a council from it; the decision reached was respected and usually considered final. Post-colonial African legal systems, though, conceive of law as a body of rules for the preservation of the state and the perpetuation of order and stability. In many places any advocacy of the overthrow of the state is considered treason and is punishable by death.

In an attempt to humanize African legal systems, in June 1981 the 18th assembly of heads of state and government of the Organization of African Unity adopted the African Charter on Human and Peoples Rights. (Their collective conscience had been pricked by Idi Amin's Uganda, Jean Bedel Bokassa's Central African Republic, and Marcias Nguema's Equatorial Guinea.) This charter sought to nudge Africa's legal systems away from their heavy colonial influences; it was somewhat influenced by African tradition with its emphasis (relative to Western traditions) on the individual as part of a group and the correlation of rights with duties. However, the Charter falls far short of prescribing new laws that could guarantee the rights, liberty and economic well-being of the majority of the people.

For instance, Article 13(1) of the Charter guarantees as follows the right to participate in government: "every citizen shall have the right to freely participate in the government of his country, either directly or through freely chosen representatives in accordance with the provisions of the law." In analyzing this proviso, we can see that the accommodating clause, "in accordance with the provisions of the law," strips the article of any meaningful human rights content. Equally, "the right to freely participate" is vague and meaningless and is of no consequence. The objective interpretation of the clause is that one is "free" only to the extent specified in the applicable national laws. Kotey argues that against the background of the African experience of one-party states, military dictatorships, and "revolutionary" autocracies, to offer the African people the right to participate in the governance of their countries within the parameters established by national law is to offer nothing at all.

In sum, African legal systems remain an impediment to the development of anarchism in Africa. The extant body of laws is capitalist inspired and is designed to perpetuate the status quo and the state system. In most parts of Africa, military dictatorships and civilian autocracies have introduced decrees and statutes that prohibit workers from organizing themselves into unions. In some countries, in fact, strikes and other forms of workers' actions are absolutely prohibited. To the extent that it sees nothing fundamentally wrong with the state system in Africa, The African Charter cannot address the issue of class antagonisms and oppression on the African continent.

And at the same time, as long as Africans continue to support the Western/colonialist-inspired legal system—and, importantly, to accept its underlying philosophies and rationale—African legal systems will remain an important obstacle to both human freedom and the development of anarchism in Africa.

THE MILITARY CLASS AND THE STATUS QUO

As discontent continues to heighten and the possibility of revolutionary action increases, the African military continues to act to maintain the status quo. Roger Murray explains military intervention as an attempt to prevent the radicalization of the people and revolutionary situations. Underlying this is the fact that the military is a central component of the national ruling class in all African countries and thus benefits from both continued government rule and from alliances with foreign investors and, in many cases, bribes from them.

The military itself perceives its function as protection of the state from both internal and external threats. This becomes obvious when one examines military coups. Professor Nnoli notes that in the January 1966 coup in Nigeria, the coup plotters had no intention, either stated or implied, of advancing the interests of the poor. "Their interest was [in] the reformation of the system, in other words, to achieve the interests of the privileged classes without imposing undue strains on the system." Yet some commentators have dubbed this particular military coup as "revolutionary." To dispel such illusions, all one needs to do is to look at the concrete economic, social, and human rights results of African military coups. The results are invariably enrichment of the military, continued impoverishment of the majority, and woeful abuses of human rights.

To summarize: as the radicalization of mass consciousness increases, the military intervenes under the guise of attempting to stop society from sliding into a state of "anarchy"—a deliberately misused catchword for chaos and disorder. What the military succeeds in doing is to temporarily roll back the gains of working people and peasants in their attempts to build better lives for themselves.

ETHNIC VERSUS CLASS CONSCIOUSNESS

The national question in African politics derives from Africa's colonial history and present-day neo-colonialism. The process of colonialization in Africa in which ethnic groups were arbitrarily regrouped into artificial political bodies has resulted in increased ethnic tensions and social and economic discrimination. Onigu Otite has noted that unequal access to political and economic resources among the various ethnic groups inevitably transforms ethnic divisions into antagonisms. Capitalist competition over control of the machinery of government plays on ethnic sentiments and sets groups against each other. Thus issues are distorted and simplified as ethnic-rather than class-based. In a paper presented to the Nigerian Anthropological and Sociological Association, Dr. Inyang Eteng exposes the successes of the Nigerian ruling class in utilizing ethnicity and religion to conceal "the class basis of most of the country's basic problems." According to Eteng, "the pernicious consequence of ethnic [consciousness] is to encourage communal hatred, corruption, violence, religious manipulation, interethnic conflict and to undermine the growth of class consciousness in favour of ethnic/state consciousness."

All of this makes it difficult for anarchism to take root in Africa because the bosses find it easy to atomize the working class by fanning the embers of ethnicity. The labor movement, for instance, becomes polarized along ethnic lines, and issues are seen through ethnic prisms. In Nigeria, when the National Union of Petroleum and Natural Gas Workers (NUPENG) called a general strike in 1994 to demand an end to military dictatorship, the leadership of NUPENG branches in the northern part of the country resisted the strike. Their reason? They felt an ethnic identification with the military dictator, who is a northerner.

RELIGIOUS AND CULTURAL FACTORS

Religion is a profound feature of African life. Long before the earliest contact with Europeans, Africans had developed religious belief systems and ritual practices. This religious belief pattern was culture-based to a great extent, and it found expression in myths surrounding life and death questions. As we saw in Chapter three, certain beliefs and rituals actually solidified the communal nature of traditional African societies. But, like all religions, traditional African religions had conservative/reactionary aspects. The preeminent place accorded the supreme being or god in the affairs of men required every member of society to act and think in prescribed manners; holding beliefs perceived to run contrary to mainstream societal mores and values led to dire consequences.

Despite the compatibility of anarchism and the traditional African way of life, African culture still frowns on any set of ideas that conflict with religious beliefs or that promote values that lie outside the so-called mainstream, especially if they involve the overthrow of the existing system. This is not surprising, however, given the close affinity between spiritual and temporal powers.

Religion will continue to be an inhibiting factor despite such material factors as capitalist exploitation, social and economic inequality, and governmental tyranny—all of which inspire despair, upon which religion, especially imported Western religion, feeds. If war is the health of the state, despair is the health of religion. Until African workers and peasants find belief systems that provides them with real hope of happiness in the here and now, they will continue to grasp at religion's false hope of happiness in the hereafter.

INTERNATIONAL SOLIDARITY

As stated earlier, anarchism as a systematic body of thought is only now beginning to find adherents in Africa. Much remains to be done. High in priority is the need to make people aware of the theoretical bases of anarchism, and to understand that anarchism is at the least as credible as other ideologies. In Africa today, as in too many other places, the word *anarchism* is synonymous with violence and chaos. But the image of anarchism will change if sufficient literature becomes available on the subject. To this end, anarchist groups in Africa need to set up a press to produce leaflets, pamphlets, and newsletters. There is also the need for alternatives to the state electronic media, which along with state- and corporate-controlled newspapers is almost the only source of information for workers at present.

Africa remains a continent where no single ideological model can be judged to have been successful. Unlike America and Europe, where capitalism and "communism" have been institutionalized and practiced with qualified and limited successes, Africa presents an historical opportunity for any ideology capable of lifting people out of their present-day misery. Existing anarchist groups on the continent must and will play an important historical role in this regard.

Africa also needs international support for its emerging anarchist groups, which have only begun to challenge the state/capitalist system. Without international support, these groups, whom the governments view simply as troublemakers, stand little chance against the organized terror of the state. Because of the alliance between the state and international capital, local ruling classes are bound to receive the support of their international collaborators in crushing any perceived threat to the status quo.

In the last resort, will the local ruling classes call in foreign troops in an attempt to maintain their privileges, as occurred in Shaba Province in the Congo in the 1960s? Of course they will. Clearly the fight against international capital and against the state system must proceed internationally if it is to have any hope of success.

7

Anarchism's Future in Africa

ANARCHISM IN A WORLD CONTEXT

The prospects for anarchism on the African continent are, in the final analysis, inextricably tied to the future of anarchism worldwide. Owing to its internationalist outlook and platform, the future of anarchism must be appraised within a global context; any attempt to localize it is bound to yield a distorted outcome. The obstacles to anarchism are, in the main, global; only their specifics are determined by local circumstances as is the case in Africa.

The crises of capitalism and, lately, marxist "socialism" worldwide have, historically speaking, assured the future of anarchism. Marx's devastating critique of capitalism as a mode of production remains overall as valid today as when Marx himself first unleashed it. But the admirable logic and systematic approach of marxism has, ultimately, been undone by marxism's internal contradictions.

Marxism's overt attachment to the state system and its structures, as the convulsions in the Soviet Union, Eastern Europe, Africa and Asia have clearly demonstrated, is a fundamental flaw. It has made a mockery of marxism's stated goals (freedom, socialism, and a classless society). The fact that there are still a few authoritarian state socialist outposts—China, North Korea, and Cuba—does not disprove this conclusion. Two outcomes in these nations seem very likely: a collapse of the state socialist ideology and system, as occurred in Eastern Europe, as these states lose their capacity to hold out on their own (Cuba, North Korea); and a transformation from state socialism to state capitalism—indeed, to a system with notable similarities to Italian-style fascism (China).

Either way, state socialism, like capitalism, is doomed. Throughout history, the overall tendency in the development of human society has been toward social equality and greater individual freedom. The pace has seemed agonizingly slow and there have been innumerable setbacks, but the overall trend is undeniable. Change has been the one constant in this development, and it almost certainly will be the one constant in the future. Given the endemic and irresolvable crises of both capitalism and state socialism, humanity's next step must almost inevitably be toward greater individual freedom and greater social equality—that is, toward anarchism, and especially toward anarchism's social expressions, anarcho-syndicalism and anarcho-communism.

Marxist "communism" is a failed experiment. It simply didn't deliver the goods (freedom, social well-being and social equality); and given its history in the 20th century, it seems obvious that it *cannot* deliver the goods.

Neither can capitalism, including the laissez-faire variety of which American "Libertarians" are so enamored. Mere elimination of the state while retaining a capitalist economy would not eliminate hierarchy, domination, and the class structure. It would not and could not lead to a truly positive freedom. The best that it could produce would be a somewhat increased freedom from external interference.

Nearly a century ago, Emma Goldman defined "positive freedom" as the "freedom *to* [do]." While gross disparities exist in the distribution of wealth and income, it seems obvious that this positive freedom will exist meaningfully for only a small number of individuals—and social equality will remain an illusion. Of course, positive freedom is a relative, not an absolute, freedom; the best that we can strive for is *equal* positive freedom. And we cannot achieve that under any form of capitalism.

So, marxist "socialism" promised (but failed to deliver) equal positive freedom, while brutally suppressing the "negative" freedoms (freedom from restraint/coercion); and capitalism has delivered only severely restricted negative freedoms. And it does not even contemplate equal positive freedom.

Humankind can do better.

THE AFRICAN CONDITION

Africa today lies prostrate, bleeding, and embattled on all fronts, a victim of capitalist and, to a great extent, state socialist ambitions. The heart-rending misery of its peoples, the conditions of abject poverty, squalor and disease in which they live, exist side by side with the wanton luxury, rapacity, and corruption of its leaders. The misery of the overwhelming majority is the result of the opulence of a few, whose stranglehold on social produce and resources, in conjunction with the power of international capital, confers to them the virtual power of life and death over the majority.[1]

Acting as middlemen and commissioned agents to multinational corporations, awarding contracts and licenses, the local business class appropriates to itself, with the help of the state, Africa's social surplus. While the local business class is very privileged in comparison with the rest of the population, it is still in a subservient role in relation to foreign capital; this, of course, is a result of the retention of the colonial economic structure in the post-colonial period.[2]

This is accompanied by coercion and massive repression of all forms of protest by the poor majority. Wages in Africa are among the worst anywhere; they are so low that they can barely guarantee basic subsistence. And the slave wages paid are perpetually "in arrears," going unpaid for months on end.

The situation in the self-styled "socialist" states is not any better. The ruling socialist party cadres and the state are, for all practical purposes, fused into one. The net effect is that the process of primitive accumulation (for the benefit of a small minority) proceeds at an even faster rate than in openly capitalist states.

Because the local capitalist class is weak and dependent on foreign capital—and thus the state is relatively stronger than in developed capitalist countries—and because in "socialist" African countries the state is the sole owner of the means of production, the struggle for state power in Africa is fierce, often ruthlessly so. This explains the ease and regularity with which African politicians, once in power, transform themselves overnight into sit-tight rulers and presidents for life, impervious to the deteriorating socioeconomic conditions of their countries.

On a global level, the relationship between Africa and the rest of the world is characterized by unequal exchange and marginalization. The process works like this: Africa is consigned to the production of raw materials and primary goods at cheap rates, while it pays for finished goods and products at exorbitant rates. Because of this unequal exchange, African nations are debtor nations that must resort to external loans. The result is that sub-Saharan African nations are indebted to a current total of well over $300 billion. This, naturally, exacts its toll on national economies. An average of 40% of all foreign exchange earnings goes to debt service charges annually, leaving little or nothing for development needs.

The 1980s witnessed the collapse of economies across the continent. In response to this, the developed countries, acting under the aegis of the International Monetary Fund (IMF) and the World Bank, formulated a scorched-earth Structural Adjustment Policy (SAP) which they forced down the throats of most African countries (see Chapter five). At the time of this writing, 35 African countries have been forced to adopt the program since 1985. It entails drastic devaluation of national currencies, the introduction of "market reforms," and deregulation of national economies, including the privatization of state-owned industries and corporations.

In the 1990s, the situation has gone from bad to worse. Negative growth rates are the order of the day, as are unemployment, triple-digit inflation, falling manufacturing capacity utilization, and a rising crime rate. And those bearing this burden are primarily the poor, workers, and peasants. Many economists, including capitalist economists, agree that Africa's debt load is, in fact, unrepayable.[3]

Against this backdrop, parts of Africa have erupted in orgies of violence, effectively spelling the beginning of the collapse of the modern nation-state system on the continent; and the rise of a new, angry generation during this chaos is an important factor in determining how and in which direction the present crisis is resolved.

However much we may want to explain away the events in Liberia, Somalia, Rwanda, Sierra Leone, Ethiopia, Mozambique, Angola, Sudan, Algeria, and, not least of all, Nigeria and Zaire, the fact is that they have their roots in the state-capitalist system and in the social and economic relations it engenders. The modern nation state system, like the empire state system before it, has failed Africa, as it has failed the rest of the world.

ANARCHISM AND THE NATIONAL QUESTION IN AFRICA

Perhaps the single most important question in the breakdown of the modern nation state is the "national question," also called the right to "self-determination."[4] The debate revolves around the rights of different ethnic groups to autonomous socio-cultural development within given states.

The national question is of particular relevance to Africa given the heterogeneity inside its component states. Many civil conflicts on the continent have been blamed, directly or indirectly, on the absence of homogenous populations. The problem is accentuated by the solutions proffered by both capitalism and state socialism: the one offers individuals and groups liberty without equality; and the other offers equality without liberty.

Common to both systems, however, is a strident appeal to patriotism, a concept that Bakunin contemptuously dismissed as the united interest of the privileged class.[5] Hiding behind patriotic appeals, the state in Africa imposes injustices and misery on its subjects, as, of course, it does everywhere else. And patriotism produces the false consciousness—in which individuals act directly *against* their own self-interest—that allows individuals to condone, indeed support, the injustice and misery caused by the state system. The state, in Bakunin's words, "restrains, it mutilates, it kills humanity in [its subjects], so that . . . they shall never raise themselves beyond the level of the citizen to the level of a man."[6]

Capitalist democracy and state socialism have both achieved the highest degree of intensified racial and national oppression. Marxist support for the principle of national self-determination is as illusory as is capitalist support of individual freedom.

G.P. Maximoff elucidates:

National rights are not a principle in themselves, but a result of the principle of freedom. No nation or nationality, as a natural association of individuals on the basis of common language, can find suitable conditions for its normal development within the confines of a capitalist environment and state organization. Stronger nations conquer the weaker ones and make every effort to dismember them by means of artificial assimilation. For that reason, national domination is a constant companion of the state and of capitalism.[7]

The national question in Africa, therefore, is only one component of the principal problem—namely, the attainment of true freedom and equality. The "national question" is thus peripheral to the real interests of Africa's working class and peasants. As long as capitalism and the state system exist, "self-determination" of nationalities means little. Maximoff notes that without fundamental change, "The right of a nation to 'self-determination' and to independent sovereign existence is nothing but the right of the national bourgeoisie to the unlimited exploitation of its proletariat."[8]

Having said that, anarchism is not in any way opposed to the rights of oppressed nationalities or ethnic groups in Africa or elsewhere. But anarchism stands above the narrow and petty ambitions associated with the quest for national self-determination. Anarchists see freedom, equality, and justice as higher goals than national interests, and the struggle for these higher goals must necessarily be international. The point, of course, is that the state, every state—no matter how national-ist—is an enemy of these goals. Maximoff explains:

> Nations which achieve their right to self-determination and which become states, in their turn begin to deny national rights to their own subordinate minorities, to persecute their languages, their desires, and their right to be themselves. In this manner, 'self-determination' not only brings the nation concerned none of that internal freedom in which the proletariat is most interested, but also fails to solve the national problem. On the contrary, it becomes a threat to the world, since states must always aim to expand at the expense of their weaker neighbors.[9]

For that reason, anarchism repudiates any attempt to solve the national question within the context of the state system. Maximoff argues:

> A real and full solution will be possible only in conditions of Anarchy, in a communism emanating from the liberty of the individual and achieved by the free association of individuals in communes, of communes in regions, and regions in nations— associations founded in liberty and equality and creating a natural unity in plurality.[10]

Anarchists demand the liberation of all existing colonies and support struggles for national independence in Africa and around the world as long as they express the will of the people in the nations concerned. However, anarchists also insist that the usefulness of "self-determination" will be very limited as long the state system and capi-talism—including marxist state capitalism—are retained.

The implications of this for Africa are immediately obvious. A viable solution to the myriad of problems posed by the national question in

Africa, such as internecine civil conflicts, is realizable only outside the context of the state system. This requires the destruction of the state system, and concerted international solidarity and revolutionary actions. The elimination of the state system is a long-term goal that will be difficult to achieve, but it is definitely preferable to the ongoing mechanistic approach as expressed in the creation of a multiplicity of unviable nation states across the continent.

ANARCHISM—THE WAY FORWARD FOR AFRICA

The relevance of anarchism to human society has nowhere been more obvious than it is in Africa. Given the multitude of problems that stare the peoples of Africa in the face, the debilitating socioeconomic conditions under which a great majority of them live, and the overall economically deprived status of Africa vis-a-vis the other continents, anarchism is really the only liberating concept capable of turning "the dark continent" in a truly forward-looking direction.

Things have gone haywire for too long; only a drastic cure can satisfy an increasingly angry, bitter and restive population stretching from Cape Town to Cairo. Conditions include the seemingly endemic problem of ethnic conflicts across the continent; the continued political and economic marginalization of Africa at the global level; the unspeakable misery of about 90% of Africa's population; and, indeed, the ongoing collapse of the nation state in many parts of Africa.

Given these problems, a return to the "anarchic elements" in African communalism is virtually inevitable. The goal of a self-managed society born out of the free will of its people and devoid of authoritarian control and regimentation is as attractive as it is feasible in the long run.

At the global level, human civilization is passing through a period of transition occasioned by the collapse of marxist "socialism" and the evidently insuperable crisis of capitalism and the state system. So, where do we go from here? As we noted earlier, all advances in human history to this point have been made possible by humanity's quest for both freedom and human solidarity. Since this craving seems a natural instinct and, as such, is not going to disappear anytime soon, it follows that the continued evolution of society will be in the direction of freedom, equality, and community.

The process of anarchist transformation in Africa might prove comparatively easy, given that Africa lacks a strong capitalist foundation, well-developed class formations and relations of production, and a stable, entrenched state system. What is required for now is a long-term program of class consciousness building, relevant education, and increased individual participation in social struggles. Meanwhile, the crises and mutations in capitalism, marxist socialism, and the state system, individually and collectively, cannot but accelerate. For Africa in particular, long-term development is possible only if there is a radical break with both capitalism and the state system—the principal instruments of our arrested development and stagnation. Anarchism is Africa's way out.

---

1. Ake, C. *A Political Economy of Africa.* New York: Longman, 1981, p. 33.
2. Williams, G. in Gutkind and Waterman, eds., *African Social Studies.* London: Heinemann, 1977, p. 176.
3. See Pius Okigbo's paper, "Africa's External Debt Crisis," presented at a public symposium, University of Lagos, November 1989.
4. Maximoff, G.P. *Program of Anarcho-Syndicalism.* Sydney: Monty Miller Press, 1985, p. 46.
5. Bakunin, M. Marxism, *Freedom and the State.* London: Freedom Press, 1984, p. 32.
6. Ibid.
7. Maximoff, Op. Cit., p. 45.
8. Ibid., p. 46.
9. Ibid., p. 47.
10. Ibid.

Bibliography

Ade-Ajayi, J.F., and Crowder, M. (eds.) *History of West Africa*, Volume 1. New York: Longman, 1976.

Afigbo, A. Ropes of Sand: *Studies in Igbo History and Culture.* Nsukka, Nigeria: Nsukka University Press, 1981.

Ake, C. *A Political Economy of Africa.* New York: Longman, 1981.
—*Revolutionary Pressures in Africa.* London: Zed Press, 1978.
—*Social Science as Imperialism.* Ibadan, Nigeria: Ibadan University Press, 1972.

Alberola, O. And Gransac, A. *Spanish Anarchism.* London: Hurricane Press, 1976.

Albert, M. (ed.) *Miguel Garcia's Story.* Orkney: Cienfuegos Press, 1982.

Ananaba, W. *The Trade Union Movement in Nigeria.* London: C. Hurst, 1969.

Anonymous. *You Can't Blow Up a Social Relationship.* Tucson, Arizona: See Sharp Press, 1992.

Appadorai, A. *The Substance of Politics.* London: Oxford University Press, 1975.

Azikiwe, N. *Ideology for Nigeria.* Lagos: Macmillan, 1980.

Bakunin, M. *Marxism, Freedom and the State.* London: Freedom Press, 1984.
—*God and the State.* New York: Dover, 1970.

Barker, R. *Studies in Opposition.* New York: Macmillan, 1971.

Berkman, A. *What Is Communist Anarchism?* New York: Dover, 1972.
—*The Bolshevik Myth.* London: Pluto, 1989.
—*The Russian Tragedy.* London: Phoenix Press, 1986.

Bohannan, P. *Social Anthropology.* New York: Holt, Rinehart & Winston, 1963.

Brinton, M. *The Bolsheviks and Workers Control.* London: Solidarity, 1970.
—*The Irrational in Politics.* Tucson, Arizona: See Sharp Press, 1993.

Bufe, C. (ed.) *The Heretic's Handbook of Quotations.* Tucson, Arizona: See Sharp Press, 1992.

Chinweizu. *The West and the Rest of Us.* NOK Publishers, 1978.

Cohen, D.L. and Daniel, J. (eds.) *Political Economy of Africa.* London: Longman, 1981.

Cohen, R. *Labour and Politics in Nigeria.* London: Heinemann, 1974.

Coleman, J. *Nigeria: Background to Nationalism.* Berkeley: University of California Press, 1971.

Crowther, M. *The Story of Nigeria.* London: Western Printing Press, 1962.

Dolgoff, S. (ed.) *The Anarchist Collectives*. New York: Free Life Editions, 1974.

Duverger, M. *The Study of Politics*. Nelson's University Paperbacks, 1972.

Ejiofor, L. *Dynamics of Igbo Democracy*. Ibadan, Nigeria: Ibadan University Press, 1981.

Fanon, F. *The Wretched of the Earth*. Middlesex: Penguin, 1961.

Fortes, M. And Evans-Pritchard, E.E. (eds.) *African Political Systems*. London: Oxford University Press, 1940.

Goldfrank, W. (ed.) *The World System of Capitalism*. London: Sage Publications, 1979.

Goldman, E. *My Disillusionment in Russia*. New York: Apollo, 1970.

Guillen, A. *Anarchist Economics*. ISEL/LA Press, 1976.

Gutkind, C.W.P. and Gohen. *African Labour History*. London: Sage Publications, 1978.

Gutkind, C.W.P. and Wallerstein, I. (eds.) *The Political Economy of Contemporary Africa*. Beverly Hills: Sage Publications, 1976.

Gutkind, C.W.P. and Waterman, P. *African Social Studies*. London: Heinemann, 1977.

Harris, R. (ed.) *The Political Economy of Africa*. New York: Schenkman Publishing, 1975.

Ilogun, E. *Christianity and Igbo Culture*. NOK Publishers, 1974.

Isichei, E. *A History of the Igbo People*. London: Macmillan, 1976.

Kropotkin, P. *Fields, Factories and Workshops Tomorrow*. New York: Harper, 1974.
—*Anarchism and Anarchist Communism*. London: Freedom Press, 1987.

Lenin, V.I. *Imperialism: The Highest Stage of Capitalism*. Beijing: Foreign Languages Press, 1975.
—*State and Revolution*. Beijing: Foreign Languages Press, 1976.
—*Selected Works*, Volumes 1-3. Moscow: Progress Publishers, 1977.

Leval, G. *Collectives in the Spanish Revolution*. London: Freedom Press, 1975.

Levine, V.T. *Political Corruption: The Ghana Case*. Palo Alto, California: Stanford University Press, 1975.

Maximoff, G.P. *The Guillotine at Work*. Orkney: Cienfuegos, 1979.
—*Program of Anarcho-Syndicalism*. Sydney: Monty Mill Press, 1985.
—(ed.) *Bakunin on Anarchy*. New York: Knopf, 1972.

Markovitz, L. *Power and Class in Africa*. Secaucus, New Jersey: Prentice-Hall, 1977.

Marx, K. *A Contribution to the Critique of Political Economy*. Moscow: Progress Publishers, 1970.
—*Capital*, Volumes 1-3. Moscow: Progress Publishers, 1956.

Meltzer, A. (ed.) *A New World In Our Hearts.* Somerville, Massachusetts: Black Thorn, 1978.

Mutiso, G.C.M. and Rohio, S.W. (eds.) *Readings in African Political Thought.* London: Heinemann, 1975.

Murdock, G. *Africa: Its Peoples and Their Cultural History.* New York: Praeger, 1959.

Ocram, A. *Politics of the Sword.* London: Rex Collings, 1977.

Offiong, D.A. *Imperialism and Dependency.* Enugu, Nigeria: Fourth Dimension Publishers, 1980.

Okafor, S.O. *Indirect Rule.* Nelson, 1981.

Onimode, B. *Imperialism and Underdevelopment in Nigeria.* London: Zed Press, 1982.

Orwell, G. *Homage to Catalonia.* New York: Penguin, 1978.

Otite, O. (ed.) *Themes in African Social and Political Thought.* Enugu, Nigeria: Fourth Dimension Publishers, 1978.

Peil, M. *Consensus and Conflict in African Societies.* London: Longman, 1977.

Purchase, G. *Anarchism and Environmental Survival.* Tucson, Arizona: See Sharp Press, 1994.

Rocker, R. *Anarchism and Anarcho-Syndicalism.* London: Freedom Press, 1988.

Rodney, W. *How Europe Underdeveloped Africa.* Enugu, Nigeria: Ikenga Publishers, 1982.

Rubin L. And Winstein, B. (eds.) *Introduction to African Politics: A Continental Approach.* New York: Praeger, 1974.

Tabor, R. *A Look at Leninism.* New York: Aspect Foundation, 1988.

Voline (E.K. Eichenbaum). *The Unknown Revolution.* Detroit: Black & Red, 1974.

Ward, C. *Anarchy in Action.* New York: Harper & Row, 1973.

Index

Aba Women's Riot 57
Abacha, Sani 61, 86
Achebe, Chinua 55
Africa
    African Socialism . . . . i, 44-46, 49-52, 72-81, 103
    Class Formation 42, 54-56
    Colonialism 39-43, 48, 54-58, 67, 73, 79, 80
        Colonial Education 93, 94
        Colonial Legal System 94-97
        Monetarization 40
    Debt 87, 88, 103, 104
    Depoliticization 80, 81
    Feudalism 28, 33
    Military Regimes 81-83, 89, 90, 97, 98
    Slavery 5, 33, 39
    Trade Unions 56-65
    Traditional African Societies . . . . i, 27-41, 95
        Age Grades 31, 32
        Anarchic Elements 27, 33, 37, 38, 41, 50
        Caste System 33
        Communalism 28-38, 41, 77
        Economic Organization 29, 31
        Jurisprudence 30
        Political Organization 29-31
        Polygyny 33
        Religion 30
        Secret Societies 31, 32, 37
African Charter on Human and People's Rights 91, 96, 97
Ake, Claude 80, 81
Algeria 46, 56, 91, 104
Alliance of Social Revolutionaries 14, 19
Amin, Idi 96
Amin, Samir 34, 73
Amnesty International 91
Anarchism . . . . i-iii, 1-23, 27, 47, 93, 99-101, 104, 106-108
Anarchism 15
Anarchism and Anarcho-Syndicalism 16
Anarchism and Environmental Survival 16
Anarchist Communism 15
Anarcho-Communism 11, 102
Anarcho-Syndicalism 11, 12, 69, 102
Andrews, W.H. 66
Angas 35

Angola 89, 104
Apartheid 63
Arabs 27
Armed Struggle 49
Ashanti 27
Authority 8
Awka 35
Azad, Ahmed 78
Azikiwe, Nnamdi 30, 31, 57, 58
Babangida, Ibrahim 59, 86
Bafayu, Paschal 60
Bakunin, Mikhail . . . . iii, 3-5, 11, 13, 14, 19-23, 105
Banbara 27
Bantu 27
Bassa Grebo 35
Bate 35
Bayankole 38
Bebel, August 21
Benin 38, 46, 88, 89
Berlin Conference of 1884/1885 39
Bevington, L.S. 11
Bini 37
Birom 35
Blanqui, Auguste 25
Bobo 35
Bohannan, Paul 34
Bokassa, Jean Bedel 96
Bookchin, Murray 14, 16
Botha, Vorster 63
Bourmedine 46
Boycott 25
Bunting, S.P. 65
Burkina Faso 35, 78
    Committees for the Defence of the Revolution 78
Capitalism 2, 6, 7, 17, 23, 24, 39-43, 50, 54, 58, 69, 89, 102, 103, 107, 108
Card, E. 84
Central African Republic 96
Chaos 9
China 5, 45, 101
Class 5, 7, 8, 55, 56
Class Conflict in Africa 82
Class Struggle 18, 19, 23, 25
Cole, G.D.H. 24
Collier's Encyclopedia 2
Communist Manifesto 19
Communalism (see Traditional African Societies)
Compaore, Blaise 78, 79
Concentration of Capital 18
Confederation General du Travail 25, 67
Congo, Democratic Republic of (see Zaire)

Conquest of Bread 15
Cuba 45, 78, 101
Dabibi, Milton 60
Dan 35
Das Capital 19
Diagne, Ablaye 87
Dielo Trouda 8
Dogon 35
Doyle, Kevin 9
Djula 27
Duke, James 63
Egypt 27, 52, 92
Ekoi 35
Electoralism 21, 23, 25, 88, 89
Emiros 55
Encyclopedia Americana 1
Engels, Friedrich 14, 48, 49
Enquiry Concerning Political Justice 13
Enugu, Nigeria 58
Equatorial Guinea 96
Eteng, Inyang 98
Ethiopia 46, 78, 89, 104
    Workers Party 78
Fanon, Franz 48, 81, 82
Federation des Bourses du Travail 25
Federation Principle 13
Fields, Factories and Workshops Tomorrow 15
First, Ruth 82
Fisher, Percy 62, 66
Freyhold, Michaela Von 76
Fulani, T.B. 64
Gadhafi, Muammar 44, 48
Galli, R.E. 54, 55, 74
Gambia 27
General Strike 25
Ghana 35, 37, 52, 56, 72, 73, 84, 90, 92
    Cocoa Marketing Board 85
    Cocoa Purchasing Company 85
    Convention People's Party 72, 73, 84, 85
Gikuyo 27
God and the State 11, 14
Godwin, William 13
Gold Coast (see Ghana)
Goldman, Emma 102
Goncharov, Leonard 41
Guild Socialism 17, 24
Guinea 35, 46, 54, 55, 67, 68, 73-75
    Democratic Party of Guinea 67, 73-75
Hall, Burton 23
Harris, Peter 81, 82

Hausa-Fulani 27, 38
Hobson, S.G. 24
Horton, Robert 31-33
Human Rights 90-92, 95, 96
Ibadan University 68
Ibibios 37
Idoma 35
Igbo 27-37
    Nri 36
    Onitsha 36
    Umu-ada 35, 36
Ijaws 37
    Brass 37
    Kalabari 37
    Nembe 37
    Secret Societies 37
    Warri 37
Imoudu, Michael 58
Industrial Workers of Africa 52
Industrial Workers of the World 52, 62, 66
International, The 65
International Alliance of Social Democracy 14, 19
International Monetary Fund 87, 88, 104
    Structural Adjustment Programs 87, 88, 104
International Socialist League 65
International Workers Association 6, 7, 9, 70
International Workingmen's Association 12, 19, 20, 22
    Basel Congress 20
    Amsterdam Congress 20, 21
Islam 39, 91, 92
Itsekiri 37
Ivory Coast 35, 92
Jamarrhiriyah 48
Jewell, Gary 62, 63
Kanem-Bornu 38
Kanuri 27
Kedi 38
Keita, Modibo 44
Kenya 56, 90. 92
Kenyatta, Jomo 44
Kerekou, Mathew 46, 88
Khran 27
Kibbutz System 47
Kikuyu 92
Kissi 35
Kokori, Frank 60
Konkomba 35
Kropotkin, Peter 4, 5, 14, 15
Kru 35
Kusaasi 35

Kwanko 35
Lagos Guardian Newspaper 60
Lenin, V.I. 65
Lever Brothers 58
Leys, Colin 76
Liberia 104
Libertarianism 102
Libya 90, 91
Liebknecht, Karl 21
Lodogea 35
Logoli 35
Look At Leninism 69
Lowihi 35
Lumumba, Patrice 44
Luo 27, 92
Maghredb 27
Majola, Sisa 66
Malawi 89
Mali 38
Mamprusi 35
Mandela, Nelson 65
Mandigo 27
Mano 35
Mariam, Menghistu 46, 78
Marx, Karl . . . . iii, 14, 18-21, 34, 48, 49
Marxist Socialism 18-22, 44, 45, 65, 68, 69, 72, 93, 101, 102, 107
Masabala, Samuel 62
Masai 27
Materialist Concept of History 18
Maximoff, G.P. 6, 105, 106
Mboya, Tom 44
McLoughlin, Conor 23
Memba 38
Mkhatshwa, Jabulani 79
Moi, Arap 92
Mozambique 78, 89, 104
   FRELIMO 78
Mugabe, Robert 91
Murray, Roger 82, 83, 97
Mutual Aid 8, 16
Mutualism 13
Nasser, Gamel Abdul 44, 45
Nationalism 42, 43, 80-83, 104-106
Nationalism and Culture 16
Nbembe 35
Ndebele 27
Negritude Socialism 44
Neo-Colonialism in West Africa 73
Neto, Augustino 44
New Encyclopaedia Brittanica 1

New Politics 23
Nguema, Marcias 96
Ngwato 38
Niger Delta 35, 37
Niger River Valley 27
Nigeria 30, 35, 47, 48, 55-61, 68-70, 85, 88, 90, 91, 97, 100, 104
    Awareness League . . . . iii, 52, 61, 68-70, 91, 100
    Axe, The 52, 68
    Corruption 85, 86
    Iva Valley Coal Strike 58
    National Council of Nigeria 60
    National Union of Petroleum and Natural Gas Workers (Nigeria) 60, 98
    Petroleum and Natural Gas Senior Staff Association 60
    Political Repression 90, 91
    Railway Workers Union 58
    Social Democratic Party 60
Nigerian Anthropological and Sociological Association 98
Nigerian Labour Congress 59-61
Nkrumah, Kwame . . . . i, 44, 46, 72, 84, 85
No Longer At Ease 55
Noimode, Bede 34
North Korea 45, 101
Nuer 35
Nye, Joseph 86
Nyerere, Julius . . . . i, 44, 46, 49-52, 72, 74, 77
Obas 55
Ocran, A. 85
Onimode, Bede 34
Organization 8
Organization of African Unity 96
Orlu 35
Otite, Onigu 98
Oyo 38
Pelloutier, Fernand 25
Post-Scarcity Anarchism 16
Private Property 6
Proudhon, P.J. 3, 13, 14, 24, 25
Purchase, Graham 16
Rawlings, Jerry 92
Religion 11, 12, 30, 99
Revolutionary Socialist League 68
Revolutionary Syndicalism 7, 9, 24-26, 62, 69
Rocker, Rudolf 14, 16
Rodney, Walter 29, 31, 33, 34
Ruge, Arnold 14
Russell, Bertrand 10, 16, 23, 25
Russian Revolution 6
Rwanda 104
Sahara Desert 27
Sand, George 14

Sankara, Thomas 78, 79
Saul, John 76
Senegal 27
Senghor, Sedar 44, 45, 72
Shaw, Ernie 66
Shagari, Alhaji 85, 86
Shona 27, 35
Sierra Leone 104
Sigmund, Paul 72
Social Democratic Labor Party (German) 21
Socialism and Rural Development 77
Socialist Register 68
Soglo, Nicephore 88
Sokoto 38
Somalia 89, 104
Somulke 38
Songhai 27, 38
Soninke 27
South Africa 1, 52, 56, 57, 61-66
  African National Congress 65, 66
  Bantustans 64
  Cape Provincial Native Congress 62
  Communist Party 62, 65, 66
  Council of South African Trade Unions 64, 65
  Freedom Charter 66
  Kincross Mining Disaster 64
  Labour Party 62, 65
  Labour Relations Act of 1981 63
  Miners Council of Action 62
  National Union of Mine Workers 64
  Port Elizabeth Strike 62
  Red Workers Republic 62, 63
  Smuts Government 62, 63
  Trade Union Council 63
South African Confederation of Labour 63
South African Industrial Federation 62
South African Mine Workers Union 62
South African Trades and Labour Council 63
Soviet Union 5, 101
State 8, 10, 15, 20-22, 25, 34
Stateless Societies 35-38
Stoicism 12
Sudan 35, 104
Syndicalism (see Revolutionary Syndicalism)
Taber. Ron 68, 93
Tallensi 35-37
Tanzania 46, 49-52, 72, 74-78
  Arusha Declaration 76
  Classes 75, 76
  National Union of Workers 76

Tanganyika African National Union 75, 76
Ujamaa 46, 49-52, 72, 77, 78
Terrorism 9-11, 91
Thomas Sankara Speaks 78
Thompson, William 13
Tiv 35, 36
Togo 35
Torch, The 68
Toure, Sekou . . . . i, 44, 46, 67, 72
Toward an Ecological Society 16
Trade Union Movement in Nigeria 57
Tuareg 27
Tukulor 27
Uganda 96
Ujamaa (see Tanzania)
United African Company 58
United Nations 74
United Trading Company 58
University of Nigeria, Nsukka 68
University of Senegal 87
Upper Volta Basin 27
Urhobos 37
Violence 9, 10
Voluntary Association 2
Warren, Josiah 13
Weitling, Wilhelm 14
What Is Property? 13
Williams, Gavin 77
Wolor 27
Workers Solidarity 9
World Bank 76, 77, 87, 88
World Conference on Agrarian Reform and Rural Development 74, 75
You Can't Blow Up a Social Relationship 10
Yoruba 27, 37
Zaire 89, 100, 104
    Shaba Province 100
Zeno 12
Zimbabwe 35, 52, 89, 90
Zulu 27, 38

ANARCHIST CONTACTS

INTERNATIONAL WORKERS ASSOCIATION

IWA Secretariat/AIT Secretariat
Po Alberto Palacios 2
28021 Madrid
Spain

ARGENTINA
FORA
c/ Coronel Salvadores 1200
1167 Buenos Aires

AUSTRALIA
Anarcho-Syndicalist Federation
P.O. Box 6778
Hamilton, NSW 2303

BRAZIL
COB
CP 7597
CEP 01064-970
Sao Paulo, SP

BRITAIN
Solidarity Federation
P.O. Box 574
London SE4 1DL

Solidarity Federation
P.O. Box 29
SWDPO
Manchester MI5 5HW

Solidarity Federation
P.O. Box 384
Preston PR1 6PQ

FRANCE
CNT
33 rue des Vignoles
75020 Paris

GERMANY
Frei Arbeiter Union
c/o Buchladen Le Sabot
Breitestr 76
53111 Bonn

ITALY
USI
Via Apulla 22
00183 Roma

NIGERIA
Awareness League
P.O. Box 1920
Enugu

NORWAY
Norsk Syndikalistisk Forbund
Boks 1044 Gimsoy
3701 Skien

SPAIN
Confederación Nacional del Trabajo
c/ Magdalena 29
28012 Madrid

Confederación Nacional del Trabajo
Ab Correos 143
46080 Valencia

UNITED STATES
Workers Solidarity Alliance
339 Lafayette Street, Room 202
New York, NY 10012

LITERATURE SERVICES

UNITED STATES

Left Bank Distribution
1404 18th Avenue
Seattle, WA 98122

AK Press
P.O. Box 40682
San Francisco, CA 94140-0682

E.G. Smith Distribution
P.O. Box 82026
Columbus, OH 43202

UNITED KINGDOM

Freedom Press
84-B Whitechapel High Street
London E1 7QX

AUSTRALIA

Jura Books
440 Parramatta Road
Petersham, NSW 2049

Dear Reader,

With the drastic decrease in the number of reviews published by newspapers and magazines, and the drastic increase in the number of books published annually, reader reviews have become very important.

If you enjoyed this book, please consider writing a reader review for your favorite e-retailer, online bookstore, or book review site.

You'd not only help the author and a small publisher, you'd help other readers discover this book.